Outrunning the Bear

How You Can Outperform Stocks and Bonds
with Convertibles

Greg Miller, CPA

Cover Design: Ramona Borthwick
Cover Photos: Greg Miller by Glenn Kulbako, Grizzly Bear by Don Johnston
Composite Photo: Brian Winchester

For more information contact:

Wellesley Investment Advisors, Inc.
20 William Street, Suite G-5
Wellesley, MA 02481

Hardcover: 978-1-939758-38-5, $29.95
eBook: 978-1-939758-39-2

Library of Congress Control Number: 2013953574

Printed in the United States of America

Sample Holdings:
The bonds given as examples are not recommendations to buy. Examples mentioned in this book include: Home Depot, AOL Time Warner, Alza, Baxter, Boston Chicken, Reebok, Starwood, UPS, Berkshire Hathaway, Google, Apple, Prospect Capital Corporation, and SPX. Before purchasing any convertible bond, investors should carefully review the bond prospectus and consult with a financial advisor who has experience in investing in and trading convertible bonds. Individual convertible bonds should be purchased based on risk tolerance, time horizons and other factors in concert with an investment professional. A complete list of securities recommended by Wellesley Investment Advisors between 11/1/1996 and 9/30/2013 is available upon request. It should not be assumed that recommendations made in the future will be profitable or will equal the performance of the securities listed. All numbers are approximate.

To

Darlene Murphy, CPA, CFP®, my business partner and President of Wellesley Investment Advisors, Inc., whose motivation, hard work, brilliance, dedication and loyalty have inspired me for over 25 years;

And

Michael Miller, our Co–Chief Investment Officer and my wonderfully gifted son, who has learned the investment lessons from our family history and driven me to continue the excellence of the firm to the next generations.

Contents

Foreword

Back in the spring of 1999, when I was finishing my master's in economics and looking for an entry-level job in finance, very few places were hiring, as most financial institutions were still licking their wounds after the 1997–1998 Asian and Russian devaluation crises that resulted in the infamous blowup of the Long-Term Capital Management (LTCM) hedge fund. A very good friend of mine who worked at the then still existing Salomon Brothers Asset Management told me that their broker-dealer Merrill Lynch was looking for a summer intern for their convertible research team. At that time, I had heard as much about convertibles as the vast majority of people had—absolutely nothing. But the work sounded pretty interesting, and I was eager to learn and get my foot in the door of finance. And so began my career in the convertible market.

It didn't take long before I fell in love with the product, and I consider myself lucky to have been initiated into this seemingly reclusive market. While my twelve-year research tenure in the market is significantly shorter than the careers of most convertible market dwellers, which often span twenty to thirty years, it has been a long enough time for me to become passionate about convertibles and learn enough about their nooks and crannies to appreciate many of their subtleties. Having met many of the market players on both the broker-dealer and investor sides over these years both in the U.S. and globally, I found that very few people who get immersed in the market ever voluntarily want to leave it unless forced to do so by the job market realities.

So what makes the convertible product and the market so great? Well, I don't want to steal Greg Miller's thunder, and as you read this book, his passion for and dedication to convertibles will be shining through page after page. Without giving too much away, I will say that in my humble opinion, a traditional convertible is a beautiful thing as it combines the best of debt and equity. I lived and breathed convertibles through the tech boom and bust followed by the 2001 recession, and then through the real-estate bubble and financial over-innovation, leading to the 2008 financial crisis and 2009 rebound. I have watched the product and the market evolve and then retrace their steps, but the convertible product has fairly consistently delivered what it is expected to do both in good and bad times, even during the 2008 crash.

I met Greg many years ago in my capacity as a convertible research analyst on one of the annual research marketing trips. By then, I had met many other convertible asset managers, most of whom have continually seemed to be on the lookout for some edge—the next market development or the next new thing in convertible structuring as a way to be ahead of the pack. I'll admit without a single reservation that Greg and his team have always really stood out of the crowd for me in their unrelenting focus on the simpler and more traditional convertible structures. While others have been chasing returns by willingly or reluctantly exploring the more complicated and exotic-looking convertibles, the Wellesley crew has stuck to their guns over so many years and has delivered impressive returns in the process, a testament to their focus on capital preservation and long-term returns.

Lastly, as I read this book, I truly enjoyed both its very informative nature and the off-beat and upbeat story-telling style, and I hope you will experience the same. With several books on convertibles out there to choose from, I think this one is the most user-friendly for individual investors who may lack the full financial and mathematical savvy of the financial market professionals, but are looking outside of the box to invest and protect their hard-earned money. Enjoy!

—Tatyana Hube
Capital Markets Analyst, Capital Markets Bureau
National Association of Insurance Commissioners
Former Head of Convertible Research
Merrill Lynch

1

Introduction

This book has three distinct concepts. But because they all help explain each other, rather than give them to you one at a time, I've sprinkled each of them liberally throughout. I hope this helps make your reading more enjoyable.

Here, then, are the concepts you'll find.

Investment Philosophy

Nothing you'll read here is more important than my investment philosophy of capital preservation. It's a lot easier to make money when you've first figured out how to avoid losing it. Throughout the book you'll find discussions and examples of winning by not losing.

How Convertibles Work

This is not a textbook. Nevertheless, after you've finished, you'll understand convertible bonds better than 98% of your peers. You'll find definitions, explanations and examples throughout.

Case Studies

Throughout history people have educated and entertained one another with stories. No exception here. Some of the stories behind convertible bonds may have a lesson or two. Others, taken from our investor newsletters, are pretty matter-of-fact but show you how we go about thinking about investment choices. All in all, I hope these case studies help make thinking about convertibles increasingly natural to you.

2

The Making of an Investment Philosophy

The investor's chief problem—and even his worst enemy—is likely to be himself.
—Benjamin Graham

Sometimes, investors (and that includes professionals—hedge fund folks, fund managers, long-time stock market players) learn things the easy way. They study and they absorb all they can about the market's past, present and future. They learn both off and on the job. More often than not, though, investors learn the hard way. As a veteran financial advisor, and the son and grandson of investors, I know a little bit about both paths.

From my perspective, our business, Wellesley Investment Advisors (WIA), is very much a family business. My business partner, Darlene Murphy, CPA, CFP®, and I founded the business in 1991 with the thought that someday, one or more of her children or mine would continue in it. Today, my son Michael is our Co–Chief Investment Officer and represents the next generation of the Miller mark on the company. The Murphy mark may take some time to materialize since Darlene's oldest child is only twelve. But our roots as a family business go far deeper than that; in fact, two previous generations of my family have heavily influenced my investment philosophy. I'd love to tell you that the path that brought us to this point was a rosy one—but like I said, sometimes these lessons are learned the hard way.

My family's involvement in the market started with my grandfather, with whom I was very close growing up. I remember sitting next to him and listening to the stories of how, in the 1920s, he built a successful chain of drugstores in North and South Carolina. Like many small businessmen, he reached the point where his business had grown and attractive offers to purchase it were coming in. He decided to accept an offer for about $200,000, which was a lot of money back when he took the offer in 1928.

Anyone familiar with history can probably tell you where this story is going: my grandfather did what everyone did when they had a large chunk of money during that time—he put the entire $200,000 in the stock market. When the crash of 1929 came along, he was totally wiped out. My grandfather lived to be eighty-nine years old, but he died a poor man; he was never able to make that money back.

That financial catastrophe had a sobering effect on my father, who was a businessman, himself. He owned a successful industrial cleaning-supply company in New Haven, Connecticut. I remember getting a call from him in 1972, and I'll never forget his news or what his plans were: "Greg, I've got some really good news. I sold my business for one million dollars. I know just what I'll do with it; I'm going to find one or two of the best mutual funds out there and put my money in that."

I was thrilled for him. He had worked his whole life to get to this moment. In the back of my mind, though, my grandfather's story haunted me. It haunted my father, too, it turns out: "Don't worry, the funds are *professionally* managed. I won't lose it the way your grandfather did," he assured me.

The mutual fund plan *sounded* good enough—they were a relatively new product at the time, and they certainly didn't seem as volatile as the stock market. My father tried to pick stable funds, including Fidelity Magellan, which was one of the most popular mutual funds on the market before 2000. But timing wasn't on my father's side: Fidelity Magellan lost almost 70% of its value between January 1973 and December 1974, and it took my father's fortune—and the hopes and dreams of so many others—down with it. By 1978, his assets had dwindled down to about $150,000. He died some years after that, without much money; just like my grandfather.

There are no sure bets in business or the market, but it seemed like my family was taking more than its fair share of lumps at the hands of the capricious world of finance. I tried to keep my own nose to the grindstone and go into business for myself in the early 1970s, just as things were going downhill for my father. I had started my own CPA firm, an uphill battle. At the time, CPAs weren't allowed to do any advertising, marketing, or outgoing sales calls; you had to wait for a prospect to call you. The pickings were pretty slim.

After thinking I was going to starve for a couple of years, a client reached out to me with an idea. He had attended nursing school, and we were meeting one day because I had just finished his tax return. After we were done talking business, he coaxed me out for a beer—over which he proposed a business plan.

His work in the medical community had given him access to information about a new development in medical imaging: the ultrasound machine. He explained that he had heard about one up and running in California, and that it took pictures for doctors to use in their diagnoses. "I think if we can get one up and running here in Massachusetts, we could make millions," he said.

I thought he sounded a little nuts! He wasn't even an RN, and I was a CPA with an MBA—I didn't know the first thing about medicine. Somehow, he talked me into maxing out our credit cards, and together we had a pot of about $12,000. That was a good start, but it wasn't nearly enough: we needed about $75,000 for the ultrasound machine. So we shopped our idea around to every bank in Boston to see if we could get a loan, and every bank turned us down—except for one. That was the foot in the door we needed to get our hands on one of the first—if not *the* first—ultrasound machine in Massachusetts.

Our operation was pretty low-tech (except for the machine, of course); we put the machine in a truck and shuttled it around from hospital to hospital and tried to talk doctors into ordering ultrasounds. We employed a part-time radiologist who would actually read the films, and the idea caught on. Over the next few years, as ultrasound grew in popularity, so did our ties with the hospital systems—we'd set up ultrasound centers where we'd be responsible for placing the ultrasound machine in the center and hiring the technicians and radiologists to read the films. We didn't stop with ultrasound, though. Around 1974, we obtained one of the first nuclear medicine licenses in the state. In 1975, we purchased a computerized axial tomography machine (back then called a "CAT" scan machine, today a CT scanner), and that idea really started to explode. Over the next ten years, we continued to grow our business, installing these imaging centers near or in hospitals all throughout Massachusetts and New York.

In the summer of 1986, I received the same type of call that had come for both my grandfather and my father: a major competitor was angling to buy our company. Things were going well, and I wasn't at the point where I was really interested in selling. The suitor had other plans; when I replied that our business wasn't for sale, he said that his company—a Fortune 500 company—planned to spend $1 billion to compete against us if we didn't sell to them. "I think you're going to find us a very formidable competitor," he said, "and so I strongly encourage you to consider our offer to acquire your company."

When I hung up the phone after that conversation, I wasn't too happy. I was proud of what we had built, and with this threat of heavy competition, I wasn't too sure what the future would hold. But I was determined to turn the situation into a favorable one, driven by my pride in the business I'd built, as much as my desire to create financially stable ground for myself after what had happened to my father and grandfather. I picked up the phone and called a friend from my MBA school days who was working at Lehman Brothers in their Mergers and Acquisitions Department,

and asked him if he would be interested in spearheading the sale
of the medical company. He flew up to Boston to talk me through
the process, and six months later, in December 1986, he was able
to help us sell the company for over $10 million.

With that milestone behind me, I was starting to think about
what was next for me—an interesting place to be when you're only
thirty-seven years old. At that time, Darlene had joined our CPA
firm, which had grown over the years to about fifteen employees.
I told her, "Darlene, I'm going to do something I've never done
before. I'm going to take off a couple of weeks, and take some time
to figure out what I want to do now that I've sold this medical
company."

I spent most of that time reflecting on my own life, particularly how it related to my family's past. I remembered how much
I had loved my grandfather, and how sad it was that the failure
of his investments overshadowed not only his business success but
also his entire life. I remembered my father, and how desperate he
had been to avoid making the same mistakes my grandfather had
made—only to fall victim to the market as well. I didn't want to
buy stocks or use mutual funds. I felt that I was too young to put
my money in bonds, because they wouldn't be paying enough. I
spent days poring over investment literature, trying to come up
with a solution that would grow my wealth without exposing me
to losing it all in one fell swoop. That's when I discovered and fell
in love with convertible bonds.

In these pages, I want to share my love of convertible bonds
with you. They're pretty straightforward, once you understand

a few basic concepts. In fact, they're so good at protecting and growing your hard-earned wealth that by the time you've finished this book, you'll be asking yourself this question: "Why don't my current advisors have me invested in convertible bonds?"

That's a very good question, indeed!

3 ————————————————

On Drawdowns and Volatility

Many investment publications, professionals, and the mutual fund industry have a well-guarded secret that they do not want the investment public to know about: drawdowns. Drawdowns are, in our opinion, the single greatest determinant of investing success or failure for most investors.

One day we Googled (it's always nice to be able to use the name of a company we invest in as a verb) "mutual fund," and over sixty-eight million websites appeared. But when we searched for "mutual fund drawdowns" (both singular and plural), guess how many websites we found? None! How can that be when drawdowns are the greatest factor in achieving investment goals?

There are many ways to measure risk and volatility in a portfolio. Some measurements, such as standard deviation and beta, are based in statistics and may not, however, be obvious to the average investor.

The concept of drawdowns is intuitive, and the calculations are not difficult either. A drawdown is defined as the loss incurred by an investment during a certain period of time, measured from its peak to its lowest point. The maximum drawdown on a mutual fund, for example, is the greatest loss experienced by a mutual fund, peak to valley, before the fund changed direction and began regaining the loss. To calculate a mutual fund drawdown, one needs to find the lowest point a fund has reached from a previous high and calculate the drop. Drawdowns are calculated as a percentage of the previous high so that they can be easily compared.

Another important concept regarding drawdowns is the "time to recover" (TTR). The shorter the TTR, the less agonizing the drawdown. However, some drawdowns, especially large ones, can take years to recover from. If the drawdown is steep enough, the investment or mutual fund may never recover!

For example, a 50% drawdown takes a 100% gain to recover, a formidable task for most funds and their investors to achieve. One of the worst characteristics of drawdowns that we've seen is that many times, they strike like tornados. They hit quickly, without warning, and cause immense damage; it's often difficult to realize their devastation until after they have struck.

We have a client. Let's call her Betty. Betty came to our offices and wanted us to place $1 million of her $3 million retirement funds in a particular mutual fund. Betty's best friend was experiencing extremely impressive results with this fund. Her friend was right: the fund Betty wanted us to invest $1 million of her retirement portfolio in was run by famous portfolio manager and investment veteran Bill Miller. Legg Mason Value Fund had a compounded annualized return of 16.4% for the fifteen years ended December 31, 2005. Bill also has the distinction of having been the only fund manager to beat the S&P 500 in each of those fifteen years!

Before continuing the discussion about invest approximately one third of Betty's retir Legg Mason fund, I asked her one simple a tion: "Betty, we have been good friends and you have been a client of our firm for many years. Looking at the portfolio we manage for you, how much could it fall, or go down in value, before you begin to question our ability as your investment advisor?"

Betty paused for a few seconds and replied, "I would not like to see my investments go down at all!" I replied to Betty that in an ideal world, none of us would like to see our hard-earned money drop in value, but the only investments we know of that never fall in value are bank accounts and money market funds. And unfortunately investments that never fall in value usually have rates of returns that lag behind inflation.

After a few more moments, Betty was able to put a figure on her loss threshold: 10%. If her portfolio went down by more than 10%, she would have "grave concerns" about our management. She continued to explain that if she did own a mutual fund or investment that fell more than 10%, she would probably want to "limit her losses," and change the manner in which her money was being managed.

Betty's response was appropriate, and typical of many investors. Although the percentage could be higher or lower than 10%, everyone has a "pain threshold": that point beyond which they cannot have their portfolio decline without considering a change—often a dramatic change—in manager selection or strategy.

Our client Betty is sixty-eight years old. We hope she makes it to a hundred, and it's part of our job to help ensure that Betty's money is around as long as she is. Her risk tolerance threshold tells us she would get nervous if her new investment in the Legg Mason fund of $1 million fell to less than $900,000. When we pointed out that despite its grand successes, the Legg Mason fund in question would have had her portfolio down to $531,800 (based on the actual drawdown of 46.82% from July 2000 to October 2002), she was quite shocked!

Betty—along with the rest of us—can't know if a mutual fund or stock will ever recover from a drawdown, let alone when. So, for Betty and most investors, "limiting losses" is just good common sense. In the event of a drawdown, without principal protection or guarantees, limiting losses translates into selling. And then Betty and other investors would be doing exactly the opposite of what they set out to do. They would have bought high and sold low. This happens to investors like Betty over and over.

Betty is very well-educated and a reasonably sophisticated investor. But this was a revelation for her. She began to realize the problem with most mutual funds and other investments. Even though there are many great mutual funds and individual stocks, typically the drawdowns will greatly exceed most investors' risk tolerance.

Gary Halbert, an investment advisor and preeminent investment newsletter publisher, said it best:

"I am as focused on the losing periods as I am on the upside potential, if not more so. Why? Because it doesn't matter how much money you might make if you were scared out of the investment due to a big drawdown along the way."

Why then do many investment publications, investment advisors and mutual funds, ignore drawdown? It's very easy to compute, so that can't be the reason. Is it because drawdown information is generally so horrific that if most investors knew the "Drawdown Truth" they would never invest in most mutual funds or equities?

Barron's magazine once did a story entitled "The Nifty 19." Now, we don't mean to pick on *Barron's*—we are faithful readers and fans. Most business publications publish similar articles almost every year. At first, it appeared *Barron's* had it right when it stated, "Rather than examine calendar-year returns, we had Lipper examine 15-year annualized total returns." (Lipper is a global research firm with over thirty years' experience providing mutual fund information and analytics to advisors, individual investors, and the media.) We agree that performance over any one, two or three years is not meaningful for long-term investors. Investment performance results must be examined in both bull and bear markets. We all remember the dot-com era of the 1990s when many mutual funds had unbelievable returns of 30% or more for periods of over three years only to totally drop to near 0% after the turn of the century.

But what *Barron's* and many other publications and mutual funds failed to disclose was the drawdown data of their "top of the heap." A drawdown or drop in the value of a mutual fund of 25% or more is a sign that the manager had poor risk controls in place.

A 25% fall in value requires an investment manager to make a 33% increase just to break even, and that does not include compensation for lost time, during which inflation or returns could have been made in alternative investments.

Believe it or not, within *Barron's* nineteen best performing mutual funds, sixteen had recent drawdowns of over 25%! Some were over 40%. And 100% of the Top 20 all had drawdowns of over 20%, an unacceptable loss for a Limited Risk Investor (again, we find similar charts in most investment publications that have the same frightening drawdown rates).

A few years before the financial crisis, we screened over 15,000 mutual funds to determine if any were investment-worthy for a Limited Risk Investor. (*Limited Risk Investor*, or LRI, is a Wellesley Investment Advisors' trademark and newsletter dedicated to an investing approach with the goal of generating superior risk-adjusted absolute returns while protecting principal.) Our criteria were simple:

1. The fund had to have earned over 10% for the last three, five and ten years. This is only reasonable because investing in mutual funds is a risky investment, with no guarantee of return of principal, so a minimum long-term return of 10% should be a mandatory requirement.

2. The fund could have had neither a calendar-year loss of more than 6%, nor more than one calendar-year loss in the last ten years. Many investors believe

they are more "tolerant" of losses than they actually are, but we have seen that numerous investors will not stay with a mutual fund if it falls more than 6% a year or has multiple years of losses.

3. The maximum drawdown could not be greater than 20% during the last decade.

4. The fund must be open to new investors.

Out of over 15,000 mutual funds we screened, we could only find two (yes, two!) that met the above criteria. If we lowered our standards on the above, to only five years' performance of 10% or greater, we could find an additional *three* mutual funds, for a total of only five! I guess we figured out why mutual funds do not discuss the "Drawdown Truth."

In our *Limited Risk Investor* newsletter, we have talked about one of the most important studies in modern-day investing, the Dalbar, Inc., study. The study revealed that the average mutual fund investor only earned 4.25% annually for the period 1983 to 2012, just over half of the S&P 500's average during the same period. Dalbar attributes this poor investor performance on the behavioral pattern of chasing returns and frequently switching mutual funds.

One of the main reasons we believe investors switch mutual funds is due to the dreadful drawdowns that prevail in most equity funds. However, research has shown that the pain of losing is greater than the joy of winning. That is to say, most investors find losing money very painful, while earning more on what they have is not as satisfying. So the most important factor, and biggest secret for investment success, is to invest in instruments that limit drawdowns and provide healthy returns.

So what should investors do if they want investments that earn more than the paltry returns of short-term bonds and other fixed income investments, yet don't want to see their portfolios devastated by drawdowns? We think the answer is Limited Risk Investing using convertible bonds and principal-protected products. Why? Because high quality convertibles generally do not have the horrendous drawdowns that most mutual funds and stocks sustain.

4

The ABCs of Convertible Bonds

The Great In-Between

Convertible bonds straddle a line between stocks and bonds. First and foremost, they *are* bonds: they carry the same promise of repayment of principal and interest as all corporate bonds do. You, as the bondholder, can sleep a little more easily at night— you're higher up on the repayment totem pole than shareholders (these bonds have what is called a "higher quality" than stocks). In addition, your bonds enjoy some of the security that stock market shareholders don't enjoy. Convertible bonds are different from other bonds in that they give holders the ability to partici- pate in the upside of the underlying company's shares, much like stocks. Investors can make the decision to *convert* their bonds into shares in order to receive greater value than the original, promised principal.

The safety of a bond and the upside of a stock. Sound interest- ing so far?

Comparing With Other Investments

Convertibles have several defining features that set them apart from the rest of the products on the market today—features that

I'll define for you right now:

- The coupon—the promised annual interest rate;

- Maturity—a defined end date for the bond;

- Calls—when the company can call back the bond, or puts—when the investor can sell it back to the company; and

- The conversion ratio.

Compared to other products, investors will note that convertible bond coupons (or interest rates) are generally *lower* than the coupon rates of the same company's non-convertible bonds. Why would investors accept these lower interest rates? Because, in return, they get the option to participate in rising stock prices, should that be the case for the stock.

Maturities vary from bond to bond. Some convertibles have a relatively short-term maturity date, say, three to seven years or so. Other bonds have a longer-term maturity of up to thirty years. This looks a tad ludicrous at first, but the bonds were written such that you can see they weren't intended to stay out that long. Many have calls and puts, which give the company and the investor rights, respectively, to buy or sell the bonds before maturity.

Finally, the conversion ratio helps determine the value of the bond using the issuer's common stock price. This ratio will be specified in the bond's initial documentation. The conversion price (simply the face amount of the bond, usually $1,000, divided by the conversion ratio) is typically set at a premium to the market price of the stock when the bond was issued—typically in the 20%–40% range, but it can vary greatly due to a variety of market factors. So, typically, buying a bond at issuance at, say, par (usually, $1,000), investors would lose money if they converted. The hope is that the underlying stock will rise. The percentage it needs to rise for conversion to be profitable is referred to as the premium. For example, a 30% premium means that if you buy the bond when it's issued and hold it until it matures, you will need the stock to rise more than 30% to get back more principal than you put in (ignoring interest you collect on the way).

The Power of the Put

While most bond investors know about calls, the puts frequently built into convertibles are so critical—and so often misunderstood—that we will ask you to read the following:

Many investors know that most bonds, except Treasuries, can be "called" or redeemed by the bond issuer at a predetermined time, prior to the bond's maturity. The main cause of a call is a decline in interest rates. If interest rates have declined since a company first issued the bonds, the issuer will likely want to refinance this debt at a lower rate of interest. The company will call its current bonds and reissue them at a lower rate of interest. Obviously, this is to the detriment of a bond investor.

But few investors know that many convertible bonds have a very special feature—they are not only callable, they are also *putable*.

A bond that is putable allows the investor to force the issuer to repurchase the security at a specified date before maturity. The repurchase price is set at the time of issuance, and is spelled out in the bond's prospectus. This is a great advantage to convertible bondholders because it can protect the price of a long-term bond against possibly rising interest rates or declines in the underlying value of the common stock.

Years ago, zero-coupon bonds were generally the only convertibles offering convertible bondholders the ability to put the bond back to the issuer. The put feature on zero-coupon bonds—and on all convertibles—is the right to sell the bond back to the company (which is obligated to buy it) on specific dates for a specified price. Although puts began as a characteristic of deeply discounted bonds such as zero-coupon bonds, today the situation has dramatically changed. Many convertibles that mature in seven years or more have put options and are putable at par. There will frequently be a series of put options at specific future dates. The exact dates, conditions, and put amounts are spelled out in the prospectus of each individual bond. While these puts are an *option* for the bondholder, it is the legal obligation of the issuer to honor them. So, in addition to the annual interest provided and the hope that the underlying common stock will increase and produce capital gains, additional safety and liquidity comes from these periodic puts.

There are two types of convertible bond puts: "hard puts" and "soft puts." A hard put is when holders receive only cash by the issuing company. Soft puts, on the other hand, can be settled by the issuer in cash, stock, or notes, or any combination thereof.

The advantage of a hard put is this: if the investor does not plan to hold the underlying stock, the market value of exercising the put is guaranteed and will not vary one iota from the market value of the stock when it is actually received from the issuing company.

If a bondholder does plan to hold the stock after exercising the put, a soft put paid in stock may be more advantageous from a tax standpoint. That is because the IRS does not consider conversion of a bond to stock as a taxable event. The holding period of the newly-received stock extends back to the initial purchase of the bond.

As you'd expect, bonds with embedded put options give the holder significant advantages. One of those advantages is that existence of a put date with a put price acts as a de facto maturity date. The yield to put will often be very different than the bond's yield to maturity. Because of this, there will be situations when the yield to put is greater than the bond's yield to maturity, and exercising the put may be more favorable to the investor than holding the bond to maturity. If the convertible is trading more on its investment value than its conversion value, the yield to put will usually be in line with the yield of a non-convertible bond with a maturity equivalent to the put date and same investment grade. Another advantage is that the existence of put options can reduce the issue's sensitivity to interest rate risk. If the yield curve is not inverted, this will tend to provide a higher theoretical floor below which the issue should not trade, reducing in turn the volatility of a putable convertible bond. A further advantage of the put options on convertibles is that if the bond is purchased properly (that is to say, employing an absolute-return strategy), holders can generally count on a positive return. **This, of course, is provided the issuing company remains financially sound, and does not default.**

For zero-coupon holders, the put feature can provide a limited check on the financial strength of the company. Coupon bondholders gain some control in the case of a company that defaults on interest payments. Although a zero-coupon bond makes no interest payments, many debenture agreements include a similar provision if the issuing company does not honor its puts. Even though interest rates are at historic lows at the time of this writing, actual zero-coupon bonds are issued far less frequently than they were in the past.

A Few Words on Convertibility

Because they are called, after all, convertible bonds, it's natural to assume that the way you take profits is by converting them into stock. Nearly everyone assumes this when they first learn about convertibles. In fact, it's quite rare for bonds to be converted except at the very end of their lives, when the holder must choose between accepting (approximately) par value in cash or the value derived from the stock price.

When the appropriate action is to convert, that action is almost always taken by a convertible professional—either a bank that deals in convertibles or one that deals in hedge funds—specializing in capturing tiny differences between the bond's market price and its stock value. It's not necessary for most convertible investors to deal with this process. Instead, you generally lock in profits (or take losses, for that matter) on a convertible bond the same way you would with anything else: You sell. Leave the actual converting to the guys who do that for a living. You're not giving up much other than a lot of paperwork, some headaches, and a little spare change.

5

The New Index, TRW

The Three Rules

Before discussing how we came to create our **Thomson Reuters Wellesley Absolute Convertible Bond Index** (TRW), we want to stress the three rules that govern our strategy and the index:

1. **Invest in convertible bonds and notes only.** Of the many convertible products, only convertible bonds and notes promise a return of principal. There are many different convertible strategies: convertible arbitrage (buying convertibles and selling stock short), "Chinese" convertible investing (the opposite of traditional convertible arbitrage), and capital structure arbitrage (trading convertibles against a company's other bonds), to name a few. There are also quite a few convertible products, for example, convertible preferreds, mandatory convertibles, and reverse convertibles. **However, convertible bonds and notes are the only convertible instruments that promise to return your principal as**

long as the company stays solvent. Many other convertible managers, funds and indexes invest in non-principal-protected strategies or products—our TRW convertible index does not. With great risk, there *can* be great reward—but there can also just as equally be great disappointment.

2. **Buy convertibles that have either no loss or only a small loss to the next liquidity event.** The liquidity events are, as you might have guessed, at these times: when the bond matures; at the call date (if there is one)—when the *company* can call the bond back from the investors; or at the put date—when the *investors* can put the bond back to the company (again, if the convertible bond has one or more puts). The value may fluctuate during the holding period, but if you purchase the bond with No Loss To Worst (also known as NLTW) when looking to the next liquidity event (maturity, the next call, or the next put), you are guaranteed return of your principal as long as the company stays solvent.

3. **Purchase only convertible bonds with short- or medium-term maturities or put dates.** Many convertible bonds today have maturity dates of five years or less. Currently, most convertible bonds that mature in over seven years have periodic puts—dates when you can get your principal back from the

company, regardless of where the underlying stock is trading. We recommend avoiding the minority of convertible bonds that mature in over seven years that do not have puts.

Keeping the average of the portfolio short- and medium-term helps avoid the risks of prolonged bear stock markets or long-term rising interest rates.

Creating the Thomson Reuters Wellesley Absolute Convertible Bond Index

"There's no reason for it. It's just company policy."

Although the Standard & Poor's 500 Index is probably the index that is the most frequently viewed by investment professionals, when investors casually discuss "the market," they usually still mean the Dow Jones Industrial Average. The Dow is a strange creation, indeed. For one thing, not a single word in its name is really accurate any longer. Dow Jones no longer exists as an independent source of information. The index includes companies that can only be called "industrial" in the most general sense of the word, and the so-called average is in fact an obscure calculation with fairly indefensible weightings. Because the index is price-weighted, a given move of, say, $1 has an equal effect on the index whether it happens in a $10 stock or a $100 one (or a $100,000 one for that matter). Thus, the fairly arbitrary decision of how many shares to have outstanding has a big effect on the index's value. The only good thing about a price-weighted index is that it's easy to understand. That doesn't make it right.

You can quickly see several of the flaws in the DJIA when you start thinking about technology. By including Microsoft and Intel a number of years ago, the guardians acknowledged that traditional manufacturing and heavy industry no longer carried the weight of earlier years, and that the most important personal-computer stocks belonged. Fair enough. But how do you then explain the fact that Apple, the most valuable company in the world these days, has no place in the Dow?

Apparently the problem with Apple is simply that the stock price is too high. Its routine moves of $10 to $20 would run roughshod over the one and two point moves—if that—of most Dow stocks. While this could seemingly be handled easily enough, by using a fraction of Apple's price, that step would call into question the entire methodology of the DJIA. And so our country's most iconic and powerful firm, in the field of perhaps our biggest contribution to the world's economy, remains outside the index that most people still call "the market."

Now, the Standard & Poor's 500, the so-called index of the professional investor, doesn't have this problem. It is capitalization ("cap" for short) weighted so that the total value of a company, which is not arbitrary, matters more than the price of its stock. But it has a different problem, one associated with its strength. The higher a stock goes, the bigger the company's value becomes, and the larger its weight in the index becomes. We call this "pro-cyclical." Buyers of the index have to put more and more of their money into the recent best performers, instead of the stocks that may offer more opportunity for those who seek value in out-of-favor companies. Some of the perceived "safety" that comes with buying large-cap companies gets undermined by the way the construction of the index chases after recent performance.

My colleague, Bill Feingold, wrote a book called *Beating the Indexes*. In it, Bill explains why the proper use of convertible bonds avoids this performance-chasing tendency and thus results in better long-term results with competitive gains in up markets and smaller (or no) losses in down ones. My partner, Darlene, and I liked Bill's book so much that we hired him to help manage our clients' money and to explain the benefits of convertibles to investors.

Before we talk about performance of various indexes, a word of caution. No one can earn what any index makes, even our TRW index. Indexes are subjective. Indexes do not have fees or trading commissions. Indexes do not hold cash. Many times, what makes up an index is not known until it has already been purchased or sold by the company maintaining the index. So, indexes should only be used as a rough guide to how a strategy works and performs, and most investors will not be able to duplicate any index. Finally, and most importantly, in the future, indexes may end up deviating a great deal from their track records. For proof of this, just look at the fall in the Dow Jones Industrial Average from 1929 through 1932.

But, let's face it. Indexes are a fact of life. People want to know how they are doing compared with the other guy. Even though all that really matters in the end is absolute performance—how much money you have—people need comparisons and benchmarks to make themselves comfortable. Cottage industries are built around the investment benchmarking and measuring process. If there's something you can invest in, there's going to be someone else who wants to know how it stacks up against something else.

Convertibles are no different. But a good convertible index needs to be representative of the traits that define the investment. It shouldn't be overly dependent on size, the way the S&P 500 is. It should be based on a more logical process than the Dow Jones Industrial Average is.

To the extent that the convertible market has come up with its own major indexes, though, it has shot itself in the foot. The most prominent American indexes are probably the Bank of America Merrill Lynch All U.S. Convertible Index and Barclays U.S. Convertible Bond > $500 Million Index. Both of these suffer from an emphasis on mega-sized deals (over $1 billion) and the inclusion of equity-sensitive structures like mandatory preferred shares and long-dated bonds that lack the favorable risk/reward profile of traditional convertible bonds. As such, they tend to track large equity indexes instead of providing a truer picture of the smaller, shorter-dated convertibles that offer a better risk/reward tradeoff but often lag in bull markets.

I've never been one to sit on my hands when I see an opportunity, where I think there's a better way of doing something that matters to me. After all, for better or worse, it's the performance of indexes that finds its way into everyday conversation about an asset class. And, I suppose, it's the performance of a well-publicized index that can help bring other investors around to falling in love with convertibles the way I did many years ago. So I decided to do something about the flaws in the convertible indexes. I decided to make an index of my own.[1]

After doing some homework, we decided that Thomson Reuters, the international information-services firm, would be the ideal partner in creating and distributing an index of convertibles managed the way I think they should be managed: that is, an index based on an investing strategy that makes the best use of convertibles' natural properties of providing protection, income, and growth, with the emphasis on protection. I wanted to make sure the index was free of all the Wall Street concoctions that look like convertibles but really aren't. Those concoctions include preferred shares, which have two major drawbacks. One is that companies can stop paying dividends on them without having to declare bankruptcy. So when times get tough, preferred shareholders get treated barely better than common stockholders do. The other problem is that preferred shares typically don't have any maturity, unlike bonds. So you have to wait for the good graces of the market to get your money back. I didn't want to have to depend on those market graces, because when you really need them, they're usually not so good.

Even worse than standard preferred shares are mandatory preferreds, a neat trick Wall Street uses to create income that isn't really there. Imagine buying a stock and being told that you have all the downside risk but only get part of the upside. You wouldn't be too thrilled about that, right? Well, that's almost exactly what a mandatory preferred share is. I say "almost" because you do get paid some income for making this seemingly lousy deal. Sometimes the income makes it a reasonable trade-off, other times not so much. But either way, your principal is not protected. So it's a non-starter as far as I am concerned.

I also didn't want any long-dated bonds in the index. Back when we started investing in convertibles, these were everywhere. But in 1994, when the Fed raised rates several times and the bond market got crushed, the convertibles market also suffered. As a result, we don't see a whole lot of twenty- and thirty-year bonds today unless they have a put option. Some companies still do offer long-dated bonds without puts. They may meet the needs of some investors, but they're not for our clients or me. Too much can go wrong in that much time, both with the bond market and the issuing company. In real life, clients need access to their funds and seldom have a twenty- or thirty-year time horizon.

Finally, even if a security has the right structure, it doesn't do you much good if you pay too much for it. Our index follows our strategy of avoiding bonds that could have significant losses even if the company remains in business. We know we miss out on some upside by avoiding high-priced convertibles, which tend to participate more fully in the gains of the underlying stock. But we will never tire of saying this: the most important thing is to minimize losses.

We devised the TRW Index, also, to follow the strategy outlined in this book. That way, the strategy would not just be a piece of market history but something investors could follow continuously. Markets change, of course, but I wanted investors to have an index to watch over a complete bull-and-bear market cycle so that they could appreciate the benefits of a unique asset class that protects downside and participates in upside. As Warren Buffett likes to say, "It's only when the tide goes out that you see who's swimming naked."

The TRW Index Strategy

Unlike most other convertible managers and funds, TRW's goal is absolute returns, not relative returns. The goals of the strategy and the Thomson Reuters Wellesley Absolute Convertible Bond Index, or TRW, are two-fold:

1. To seek an absolute return; and

2. To outperform bonds and stocks over full market cycles.

Relative-return managers and funds are usually focused on beating an index. Absolute-return strategies allow for real, measurable returns that mean something for *your* investment. While a relative-return manager might put a spin on a bear market by saying that your investments kept pace with other underperforming options, rather than losing money, an absolute-return strategy would never put you in that position, because the goal is performance, not keeping pace. As one of our outside directors likes to say, "You can't buy groceries with relative returns!"

The second goal of the TRW index is to outperform *both* **ordinary bonds and stocks over complete market cycles.** This means that the strategy is intended to function over complete market cycles, aiming for solid performance during a bear market (when the market is down) and a bull market (when the market is on a run). By not losing money during a bear market, or not losing much money, there is less pressure to perform during the bull market. Market cycles, on average, have occurred about every six years, and as you can see from the chart on the following page, their impact is felt throughout each decade.

A bear market is defined as a 20% or greater fall in the stock market (usually defined by the Dow Jones Industrial Average [DJIA] or S&P 500 index). In the chart we used the DJIA, because the S&P 500 index did not come into being until the 1950s.

Not surprisingly, as you can see from this chart, every decade for over one hundred years has had at least one bear market. What is surprising to many investors is that most decades have two or three bear markets! Yes, the 1920s only had one bear market, but the DJIA fell a walloping 89%! It took about twenty-five years for stock investors to get back their principal (if they stayed in that long). I think the following chart is the most important chart in

Convertibles as an Asset Class

Year	Number of Bear Markets	Percent Decline in DJIA
1900s	3	46%, 49%, 27%
1910s	3	24%, 40%, 47%
1920s	1	89%
1930s	3	23%, 49%, 41%
1940s	1	24%
1950s	1	19%*
1960s	3	27%, 26%, 36%
1970s	2	45%, 27%
1980s	2	24%, 36%
1990s	1	21%
2000s	2	38%, 53%

*Since the S&P 500 did have a 22% decline in 1957 many investment professionals consider the decade to have had a (single) bear market.

this book because if it were not for regular, continual, periodic bear markets, convertible bonds would not hold such a unique value proposition.

It's important to note that the TRW index does not try to outperform equities during bull markets. In fact, it will generally lag the performance of stocks during up markets. But because it has the goal of outperforming equities during bear markets (and hopefully not losing much or any principal during a bear market), it can underperform stocks during bull stock markets and still end up outperforming them over complete market cycles. Simple math says that losses are very hard to make up. If you lose 50%

of your principal, you then need what's left to gain 100% just to break even. The TRW index will usually also underperform fixed income during bull bond markets, but outperform regular and non-convertible bonds over bear bond markets.

---

[1]TRW is the Thomson Reuters Wellesley Absolute Convertible Bond index ("TRW"). The Index is a joint venture between Thomson Reuters and Wellesley Investment Advisors. TRW is intended to represent a strategy with the goals of absolute returns and outperforming both equities and fixed income over complete market cycles deploying convertible bonds. WIA has discretion over the selection of index constituents and their weighting in the index.

No representation is being made that any account will or is likely to achieve profits or losses similar to those shown. One of the limitations of hypothetical model performance results is that they are prepared with the benefit of hindsight. There are numerous other factors related to the markets in general or to the implementation of any specific trading or investment strategy that cannot be fully accounted for in the preparation of hypothetical performance results, and all of which can adversely affect actual trading results. Results shown are for the index strategy, not actual performance in the TRW hypothetical Index. Returns shown are not indicative of actual performance for any client account. A direct investment in an index is not possible.

6

Performance Records for the TRW

We've talked about investing for absolute returns versus relative returns, and the problem with indexes. Now let's talk about performance numbers.

The performance record that follows is an example of a limited risk investment strategy at work (in keeping with the TRW index).

	Performance Record – 13 Years		
Year	Thomson Reuters Wellesley	S&P 500 TR	V0A0
2000	18.1%	-9.1%	-11.7%
2001	8.1%	-11.9%	-4.0%
2002	5.1%	-22.1%	-5.0%
2003	17.3%	28.7%	25.8%
2004	7.4%	10.9%	8.5%
2005	2.0%	4.9%	-0.3%
2006	12.0%	15.8%	12.8%
2007	7.8%	5.5%	4.1%
2008	-17.7%	-37.0%	-33.0%
2009	34.0%	26.5%	47.2%
2010	12.1%	15.1%	16.5%
2011	-1.1%	2.1%	-3.4%
2012	10.1%	16.0%	14.4%
2000 – 2012	8.2%	1.7%	3.8%

Please see descriptions of indexes in the appendix. All numbers are approximate.

In the table on the preceding page, you have comparisons of the TRW strategy versus the S&P 500 and the Bank of America Merrill Lynch (V0A0) convertible index on the far right.

In bull markets, such as in 2003, you can see that the S&P far outperformed the composite numbers for the TRW. In 2003, for example, the S&P went up nearly 29%, while the TRW composite only saw gains of about 17%. Similarly, in 2006, the S&P went up 16%, while the TRW index went up only 12%. We've been candid about the fact that stocks and other equities *can* outperform convertibles—when things are going well.

As we know, things do not always go well.

Indeed, if you were to look at the flip side—bear markets— the benefits of a convertible bond strategy similar to the TRW become clear. When the S&P went down 9% in 2000 and the Bank of America Merrill Lynch convertibles index went down nearly 12%, the TRW index actually went *up* 18%. And that's in a bear market! Similarly, in 2001, when the S&P went down almost 12% and the convertibles index fell almost 4%, the TRW index *gained* 8%. In the third year of that bear market, 2002, the S&P fell 22%, the convertibles index fell almost 5%, and the TRW index rose over 5%. Because we were able to make money during the bear, we were not beholden to crossing our fingers during the bull, hoping for larger than average returns.

Why do convertibles outperform stocks in bear markets? The answer is really pretty simple. It can be very hard to hold onto an investment when you have no way of knowing when—if ever—you might get your money back. That's the big problem with stocks.

With convertible bonds, bought at disciplined prices, you know when you get your money back, even in bear markets, as long as the issuing company remains solvent. That's all there is to it.

Being able to hold on through the bad periods leads directly to consistent, positive returns over long periods of time. That's the mantra, and you can see the evidence. If you look at the entire period, there are only *two* down years—in 2008, one of the worst market crashes in history, and in 2011. The TRW index composite investments *did* fall almost 18% in 2008, but that's far less than the 37% drop the S&P experienced, and also much less than the 33% loss of the convertibles index as a whole. And when we look at the *annualized* returns of the entire period going back to 2000, the TRW index outperformed both the S&P and the Barclays bond index.

While it is important that the TRW index perform well over any given year, absolute-return investing using this strategy also entails aiming for positive performance across entire market cycles. We simply cannot overemphasize the importance of having an investment strategy that aims for performance in any and all market environments.

It's easy to make money during a bull market—everyone can show positive returns when a market is in the midst of an incredible run. But what's more important is how you fare in a *bear* market. How far you fall influences the bottom line in that you lose not only money, but also *time*. For most investors, the next bull market will be spent recouping ground lost during the last bear market. Investors in this strategy can instead focus on add-ing to a solid foundation of positive, or at the very least, *preserved* returns from the last bear market.

Performance Record – Over Complete Market Cycles

As of December 31, 2012:	Thomson Reuters Wellesley	Barclays Agg. Bond	S&P 500 TR	B of A Merrill Lynch V0A0
Since Jan. 1, 2000 (2 market cycles)	8.2%	6.3%	1.7%	3.8%
10 Years (2 bull, 1 bear market)	7.6%	5.2%	7.1%	7.3%
5 Years (1 market cycle)	6.0%	5.9%	1.7%	4.9%
3 Years (bull market only)	6.9%	6.2%	10.9%	8.8%

Please see descriptions of indexes in the appendix. All numbers are approximate.

Where things really start to get impressive (and persuasive) for the TRW index is when we start to look over complete mar-ket cycles. Looking back over five years, or one complete market cycle (a bull and a bear market), we can see that the TRW index saw a 6% annualized return (comparable to the Barclays' bond index, but keeping in mind that the period included a horrific bear market) whereas the S&P only returned 1.7% and the Bank of America Merrill Lynch convertible index returned 4.9%.

Over *ten* years, which only includes one bear market (meaning that the statistic is more generous towards up-equity, or bull, markets—keep this in mind when we reveal the results!), the TRW index earned an annualized 7.6%, outperforming the S&P, which was at 7.1%. The V0A0 convertible index was in the hunt at 7.3%, and the Barclays bond index returned 5.2% annually.

Finally, over two market cycles, or comparing data since January of 2000, the TRW index is far and away the best performer of the group. The TRW index saw a 8.2% return, whereas the convertibles index and the S&P only came up with a 3.8% and 1.7% return, respectively, and the bond index returned 6.3%. For the S&P, in particular, 1.7% is a pretty damning figure, dismantling the popular opinion that over the long term, stocks should be your surest bet. After looking at these numbers, you may no longer be convinced!

This strategy can perform *very* well for investors who want to invest over the medium term (again, a full market cycle, on average six years) and are far-sighted enough to understand that the long term will inevitably include many up and down markets. When you factor in the damage that the inevitable bear markets can do, the surprising gains of the bull are no longer that impressive. On the contrary, the best they are probably doing is making up ground that you might not have lost in the first place had you considered investing with the TRW index in mind.

7 ———————————

Convertible Stories:
The Home Run and the Strikeout

Hitting a Home Run With Home Depot

Though it's hard to imagine, now that it's literally a household name—perhaps the gold standard in that industry, back in 1996, Home Depot was not a Dow Jones Industrial Average company and was much smaller than it is today. The TRW index contains a lot of smaller and mid-cap companies, because if they do perform well, the rewards are often far greater than with so-called blue chips. In November of 1996, Home Depot was one such company that caught our eye—the stock was selling for about $17 a share, and we thought it had wonderful prospects for growth.

No matter how attractive the company appeared, however, we are risk-averse investors with risk-averse clients. So even though we liked the stock, we bought the convertible bonds. At the time, the convertible was a five-year bond, which meant that the principal repayment was due on October 1, 2001 (see chart on the following page). The company, however, had a call on the bond in three years—meaning that Home Depot had the right, but not the obligation, to buy back the bond from the investors at a set price. We expected the company to call the bonds if the stock performed well. Along the way, investors would receive a 3.25% annual interest payment, whether or not the stock lived up to their expectations. While we liked the idea of getting paid the coupon while we waited for the stock to perform, we would not have bought the bonds if we hadn't expected big things from the company.

Home Run Example: Home Depot

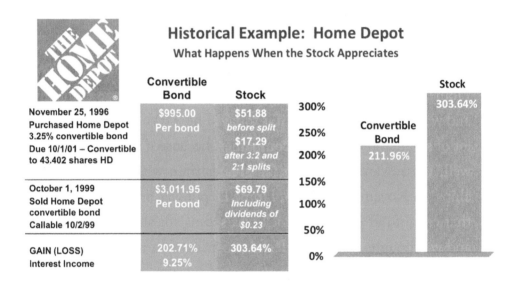

Historical Example: Home Depot
What Happens When the Stock Appreciates

	Convertible Bond	Stock	
November 25, 1996 Purchased Home Depot 3.25% convertible bond Due 10/1/01 – Convertible to 43.402 shares HD	$995.00 Per bond	$51.88 before split $17.29 after 3:2 and 2:1 splits	
October 1, 1999 Sold Home Depot convertible bond Callable 10/2/99	$3,011.95 Per bond	$69.79 Including dividends of $0.23	
GAIN (LOSS) Interest Income	202.71% 9.25%	303.64%	

Assume an investor purchased these bonds at $995.00 per bond on November 25, 1996. With Home Depot shares trading at $17.29, convertible investors were entitled to about $750.00 worth of Home Depot stock (43.402 shares). Obviously, a bondholder wasn't going to convert the bonds on Day 1, as doing so would mean losing nearly $250 ($995 minus $750). So a buyer of the Home Depot bond needed the stock to go up about 33% before the bond started to deliver significant upside.

Home Depot delivered, and then some. Home Depot *did* exercise its right to call the bond after three years. At that point, the stock price had appreciated from $17.29 a share all the way up to the equivalent of $69.79. Factoring in dividends and splits, the stock had gone up more than *300%* over the three years. Because the bond was convertible into 43.4 shares of Home Depot, the bond appreciated over that period from $995.00 to $3,011.95 per bond. If you sold the convertible bond at $3,011.95, over that three-year period the bond paid about 9.75% interest, and the bondholder received a great long-term capital gain of 202%— and a total return of 211%.

Compare this gain with that of the stock price. An investor who held Home Depot's *stock* rather than its convertible bonds over that three-year period and sold the stock on the same day that they sold the bond on the open market—they would have made about 303%.

While it's easy to look at those figures and think that the better choice would have been to buy simple shares of stock, we know from experience that that's definitely not the case for risk-averse investors. Although the stock will perform well in certain periods, it's not always going to perform well. And investors are not always right about which stocks are or aren't going to perform well, let alone when they will rise or fall. There are no sure bets, except the certainty that for every home run, there's a strikeout lurking in the shadows.

Striking Out With AOL Time Warner

If you want to talk about high expectations falling flat, consider the AOL Time Warner merger. Touted as a game-changing blockbuster before it happened, the combination went down in history as what many consider to be one of the worst business deals of the dot-com era. The precipitous drop in values of these companies was enough to make even the steadiest investor's head spin. This makes it a perfect example to illustrate a near worst-case scenario. Here we can see how, even in dire conditions, convertible bonds can still protect investors and deliver acceptable returns.

Most investors were wrong about investing in AOL Time Warner. AOL was one of the hottest Internet companies around the turn of the last century, and Time Warner was a media powerhouse. Many of the "experts" thought the stock would skyrocket—from $40 per share to over $100 per share over the short term. Considering that during the dot-com boom, many Internet companies were doubling and tripling in a matter of *months*, these predictions seemed reasonable enough.

AOL Time Warner had a convertible bond. In November 2000, some investors opted to buy them at $501 per bond, rather than investing in the stock (see chart on the following page).

This was a somewhat unusual security; while bonds typically pay interest, the AOL Time Warner bond was a 0% convertible bond. That was fine since investors were buying the bond partly because they had the right to convert it into 5.834 shares of AOL Time Warner. So, conservative investors settled down with the bond, not seeking to convert it quickly because the stock was

Strike Out Example: AOL Time Warner

Historical Example: AOL Time Warner
What Happens When the Stock Depreciates

	Convertible Bond	Stock
November 30, 2000 Purchased AOL 0% convertible bond Due 12/6/2019 – Convertible to 5.834 shares of AOL (Put on 12/6/2004 at $639.76 per bond)	$501.25 Per bond	$40.61 Per share
March 28, 2002 Sold AOL 0% convertible bond	$548.75 Per bond	$23.65 Per share
GAIN (LOSS)	9.47%	(47.16%)

	Convertible Bond	Stock
20.00% 10.00% 0.00% -10.00% -20.00% -30.00% -40.00% -50.00%	9.47%	(47.16%)

$40.61, they would only get $236.00 in the conversion, less than half of the bond price. These investors were ready to sit tight and hope the stock would go up $100 or more.

The bond was due to mature on December 6, 2019. Given that we're *still* not anywhere near that date at the time of this writing, it might have looked insane to agree to those terms in November of 2000 when many bought the bond. A lot could happen in those nineteen years, to be sure—and not all of it would necessarily be good news, as time and the market would eventually prove. But there's one feature (and advantage) of many convertible bonds that shortens this time frame and makes investing a lot safer.

Most convertible bonds today that have long-term maturities of over seven years have the *"put"* feature we briefly discussed earlier. A put feature allows the holder of the bond—the investor—to "put" the bond back to the company every one, three, or five years (or on some other schedule that is spelled out in the bond's prospectus). Most puts do turn out to be every five years, but it's possible that they could be annual. The benefit of a put feature is that it gives bondholders the guarantee of a fixed price on the date of a put. In effect, it is giving long-term bondholders short-term maturities in which they can get their principal back, often with interest. So if the value of the common stock is depreciating, there can be great protection in the value of the put feature.

Puts have gained in popularity over the years, probably because of the protections they offer investors. The first convertible bond to have such a feature was Waste Management, underwritten by Merrill Lynch in 1985. The idea of puts on convertibles became so popular that Merrill Lynch continued to offer convertibles with put features, and the rest is history. The reason for the popularity is obvious: bondholders get that guaranteed moment when they're able to put the bond back and become whole again, regardless of how low the underlying stock has fallen. The more attractive the bond is to the holder, the more the company issuing the bond will benefit; they gain increased liquidity from increased sales of these bonds. It's a quid-pro-quo situation, in which all parties benefit.

When investors bought the convertibles of AOL Time Warner on November 30, 2000, they could read the prospectus and see the various put dates and amounts on the bond. The next put was on December 6, 2004. That put price was $639.76. Buyers knew that if they held the bond for four years, and as long as AOL Time Warner was solvent, they would be able to put it back to the company on December 6, 2004, for $639.79—a 6% annualized return.

You probably remember what happened next. AOL Time Warner's stock price absolutely plummeted over the next eighteen months—the experts were all wrong. The market had crashed. It was the end of an era for Internet stocks, the bursting of the dot-com bubble. Over those next eighteen months, the stock of AOL Time Warner fell 47%.

But that was just the *stock*. Over those eighteen months, the value of the convertible bond actually went up from $501 to $548, or 9.5%. Why would this be? Investors knew about the put features, and knew that in less than five years, they could put the bond back to AOL Time Warner for $639. In this situation, investing in convertibles turned out a lot better than investing in stock. This is the idea behind convertibles. While they don't go up *as much as the stock* when the stock goes up, they usually fall *much less* if the stock goes down.

Some investors actually ended up selling the bond in March 2002, over two years before the next put date. A lot of people asked us why these bondholders were selling it and not holding on until the put date.

Here's what we told them.

The first reason is because at that point, it was what is called a "busted convertible." While there is no formal definition for a "busted convertible," the term is generally used to describe convertibles trading below their issue prices, with the underlying stock lower than it was at the time of the bond's issue and sub-stantially lower than the conversion price. In the case of AOL Time Warner, the stock was down to $23.65 a share. If investors ever wanted to share in capital appreciation from this stock, they would need it to get up to $86 a share before they would earn more than approximately 6% annualized. In percentages, that fig-ure represented a meteoric 263% increase—something that clearly wasn't going to happen, at least not in the near future.

When it came time to make the decision to sell the bond, for many holders it *wasn't* because they were worried that AOL Time Warner would go out of business. The bottom line on why inves-tors sold in March 2002 was that they thought they could deploy that capital someplace else and make more than the 6% increase that the bond appreciation would get them at the next put date. If these investors were in a market where they didn't see other con-vertibles that they thought could do better than 6%, they probably would have continued to hold the bond until the put date. When they sold the bond for $548.75 per bond, they realized a gain of 9.5%.

Projecting out a little, though, we see it's interesting to observe that other investors *didn't* sell the bond. In fact, consider the case of investors who kept the bond until November 9, 2009, five years after the first put date: how did they make out? These investors, holding the bond for five years past that first put, would have made 6% per year. The stock, meanwhile, continued to flounder at around $29 per share. Almost ten years after the bond was issued, equity owners would have still been significantly underwater (when our investor bought the bond, remember, it was at $40 per share).

The results of these two scenarios attest to one of the main benefits of convertible bonds, as we view them. Even though it seems like a tame gain for Home Depot convertibles holders compared to the stock market (if we can call tripling money in three years tame), the convertible bondholders were *never* exposed to the full volatility of the AOL Time Warner shareholders—nor *would* they have been exposed to a situation like that had Home Depot stock disappointed them. We can look at market trends, past performance, and all of the little tips floating around in the financial news, but we can never be certain that disaster won't strike. When convertible bonds are the cornerstones of your investment strategy, you're going to be poised to come out a winner—or at least in relatively good shape—compared to a lot of victims of the unpredictable market.

8

Absolute-Return Investing

There are many good reasons to add convertibles to your investing arsenal. But perhaps the best comes from the crowding and herding that comes from a market dominated by indexers and closet indexers.
—Bill Feingold, *Beating The Indexes*

The TRW index strategy advocates a focus on *absolute* returns as opposed to *relative* returns. This is a key concept often overlooked by investors, who are wowed by (or confused and shut down by) graphs and charts promising that their investments could perform favorably based on the fact that those investments beat the indexes in past years.

The problem with aiming for relative returns is that when you're talking about investing your hard-earned money, you shouldn't be concerned with how other people are doing. This goes hand in hand with what we talked about in the last chapter and elsewhere, when we warned you against the dangers of market timing, chasing performance, and trying to keep up with the Joneses. The bottom line is that *your* money should perform well for *you*—not against somebody else's standards. The reasons for this are more than philosophical: Your retirement planning should be based on the performance of your funds, and it isn't going to do you a bit of good if your portfolio is worth less money but still *worth more than the average portfolio* in a bear market. You may need that cash!

For this reason, our strategy advocates absolute returns. We want you to be able to perform well and perform well consistently over market cycles based on your initial investment, not someone else's.

Additionally, there are other problems at play when investors talk about beating indexes. Those problems are inherent in the way that the indexes are structured. Although they can be presented to investors by investment managers as tools for comparison, the reality is that they are far less objective than investors are led to believe.

In Bill Feingold's book, *Beating the Indexes—Investing in Convertible Bonds to Improve Performance and Reduce Risk*, he does a great job of unpacking the problem with indexes. The people who run the indexes aren't independent agencies beholden to no one. The Dow Jones Industrial Average and the Standard & Poor's 500 index, for example, are both corporately owned by multibillion-dollar corporations (News Corporation and McGraw-Hill, respectively). That means that there are people behind the curtains of the rating agencies who may have a vested interest in certain companies. And even if they *don't* have a vested interest in the companies they are rating, they're still operating on conjecture and opinion. There's not really much rhyme or reason to these indexes—most of them don't really mean very much at all. They are interesting to watch, and can offer benchmarks for performance, but they are by no means the be-all and end-all in investing, nor should investors assume that just because a certain stock is performing well on any given index that it's a sound investment for them.

Capitalization-weighted indexes (like the aforementioned ones, and many others) are flawed in their construction. They are, as we noted previously, pro-cyclical. This means that they overweight the recent best performers and underweight companies that they perceive to be "laggards." It's easy to overlook this flaw when your stock is one of the best performers at the moment, but thinking back to the recent crash—do you think investors in Lehman Brothers could complain to anyone when that company, and that company's stock, went belly up? No, they couldn't, nor could indexes containing Lehman. They had no cause to be knocking down the door of the Dow Jones and the S&P, claiming that someone owed them their money now that their star performer had gone under. Simply put, over-weighted stocks, and the indexes that rely on them to measure performance, are dangerous to investors.

In the eyes of these types of indexes, convertible bonds may seem like those laggards. Convertibles will tend to underperform indexes like the S&P in certain years, especially in a bull market. Common indexes don't take into account the unique risk/reward profile of convertible products, and may weigh them unfavorably against equity-sensitive products (or even other convertibles, like convertible preferred shares, which do not offer put date protection or maturities) that have recently appreciated or seen major gains in their underlying stock.

So on one hand, we've got the subjectivity of the people behind the indexes, which should be your first clue that maybe they're not the most reliable things on which you base performance. And on the other, we have the basic fact of the matter that beating an index doesn't necessarily mean that your return is going to be what you'd hoped for.

This is why we've developed the TRW index: it's built for limited-risk investing over long periods of time. Convertible bonds are uniquely positioned to perform well over different market environments; not simply beating the indexes and providing relative-return gains, but using a strategy similar to the TRW, they can provide absolute returns that far and away beat what Feingold calls the "biases and mediocrity of index investors."

When you invest in convertibles, you are much less sensitive to market fluctuations—unlike those who are racing against time and an index. If you, or your investment advisor/manager, research and purchase convertibles properly, then you have far less to worry about and negotiate when compared to stock market investors who are reaching for a performance based on the market index. One of the major reasons, again, is that convertible bonds have built-in liquidity events—puts and fixed maturities—that you can take advantage of. These are points in time when you know, as long as the issuing company is solvent, you can get your principal back. Think back to the Home Depot and AOL Time Warner situations in the previous chapter. In the case of AOL Time Warner, it was about being able to get out with your shirt still on; in the case of Home Depot, it was about being able to take advantage of a majority of the underlying stock's stellar performance. When you invest in the stock market, you've committed your funds to a time horizon that you can't really put your finger on. You might have an intention of only making a short-term investment, but the reality of market fluctuations might dictate that you'll need to keep your money in the market much longer in order to avoid a catastrophic loss. On the other hand, you might think that you have a long time to make money with the stock, but financial realities (and market behavior) might dictate otherwise.

This is not true of convertibles using the TRW index strategy. The uncertainty of time horizons is greatly diminished: convertibles offer investors the comfort of knowing that principal *will be* returned, and also, when it will be returned. This enables decision processes that are profoundly different. Investing in convertibles with an absolute-return strategy produces results that are going to mean much more than the numbers of investors who are only chasing *relative* returns.

9

Why Haven't I Heard of Convertibles?

In the wake of the recent lack of trust of the financial industry and certain fund managers, it's conceivable that consumers might think that convertibles are a newfangled, too-good-to-be-true, Wall Street invention. Nothing could be further from the truth.

Actually, convertibles have been around since the 1800s, when they were used to finance the railroads—a cornerstone of American infrastructure—both at that time and today. Still, they're not necessarily the most talked about product on the market, and that's partly because you really need someone with experience in convertibles to guide your investments through the process successfully. Brokers and other advisors might not possess knowledge about all the features available in the bond (such as puts) that make it a valuable commodity, and therefore might unintentionally mishandle the investment or shy away from it entirely. We meet otherwise knowledgeable financial people all the time who admit, a bit sheepishly, that they know nothing about convertibles.

One of the main reasons that you probably haven't heard much about convertibles is that Wall Street has never figured out how to classify them. This is a problem because the culture of professional investment management revolves around buckets to fill and boxes to check.

We are often asked, "Are convertibles bonds or stocks? Where do I put them?"

It's ironic that one of the great benefits of convertibles—that they can serve so many investment needs—actually works against them because of this mechanical classification issue.

That doesn't mean, however, that they aren't a good investment. Indeed, they offer a relative safe haven for today's investors, who are dealing with unprecedented low interest rates and high volatility. And the fact that professional allocators eschew convertibles because they don't fit neatly in predefined categories means they're available to you at more attractive prices than they probably should be.

Also, even in (perhaps especially in) a bear market, it's critical to invest. People still need the potential for growing their income—it's never advisable to pull all of your money away from financial products available to you in favor of stuffing it in your mattress. You're not going to get growth that way, and security in the face of inflation isn't going to happen that way, either. Although they're obviously not on the same risk level as an FDIC-insured savings account, convertible bonds can represent a comparatively safe bet for conservative investors: unless the company becomes insolvent, it promises the full return of your original investment—as long as you got it for the right price and didn't overpay. Bottom line? Just because you haven't heard much about convertibles doesn't mean you shouldn't start listening now.

10

Convertible Stories:
Alza (2004)

One of our favorite convertible bonds that we got involved with was a small pharmaceutical company called Alza Corporation. About twenty years ago, we noticed this maker of drug-delivery systems, which was founded in 1968. Alza (named for its Uruguayan founder, Dr. Alejandro Zaffaroni) employed a considerable workforce, though not a large number by any means when compared to large-cap, blue-chip companies. Alza had 10,000 employees, developing its drug-delivery systems and changing lives through medical advancements.

Like Home Depot, we weren't looking for a hulking blue-chip stock. We were looking for a small company with potential—a good product, a good balance sheet, and good buzz. That's where the real money is to be made. We've also always had a bias towards buying convertibles in the medical or biotech fields, because they're either likely to find a cure or an advancement themselves, or get bought out by a larger company who wants to acquire their knowledge, patents, personnel, and so on.

We started to buy the Alza convertible for clients on September 30, 1994. It was a zero-coupon convertible that didn't mature until July 14, 2014, so it was a twenty-year bond. When we purchased the bonds, we bought them at $340. Our interest in Alza paid off when, in May of 2001, they were acquired by giant Johnson & Johnson for a stock deal worth $10.5 billion. We sold out of the bond for just about all of our clients on February 29, 2004, about ten years later, for $1,372—a 300% return on their money.

Our experience with Alza demonstrates the importance of buying the right product at the right price. While you can't make a career making bets on stocks, buying a convertible bond issued by a strong company with good prospects means that when that company is acquired by a more successful company and its star rises, you're well-positioned for a nice return on your investment.

11

An Investment for All Seasons

Who Should Invest in Convertibles?

There are a lot of opinions out there about what type of investment product is right for each type of investor. You've probably heard some of the more common-sense stuff: Investors who need to keep their money relatively liquid and accessible for whatever reason should avoid long-term investments. Those who can afford to be "away" from their money for a while can try longer-term products, like bonds with long-dated maturities. Investors with a high risk tolerance might do well in the stock market. Risk-averse investors are often steered towards "safer" products, like short-term Treasuries or money-market accounts.

But what about convertible bonds? Because convertibles are a hybrid investment product, it makes sense that *many* different types of investors might be a good fit for them. Remember, while they might seem exotic or foreign to most people outside the financial sector, they've existed as an asset class for over 150 years. This doesn't mean that they're right for every investor, of course. But it does mean that they might be right—and safe—for you. Definitely, in the case of following the strategy deployed by the

TRW index, they are a necessary and extremely valuable component of watching your returns grow as they are protected.

Growth for Bond Investors

One group of investors who might find that convertibles are a good fit for them are those who may already have exposure to the more typical bond products. These include the following: Treasury bonds (fixed-interest government bonds that usually mature after ten years or more, and pay interest semi-annually); municipal bonds (securities that are government-backed, but are issued by a state, municipality, or county—something that functions on more of a local level than Treasury bonds); and "straight" corporate bonds (a higher risk than government bonds, typically, and issued by a corporation—a different, more stable product than stocks, of course). These bond investors may have been drawn to these types of products initially because of their substantially lower volatility compared to stocks. Convertibles are probably a good fit for them.

Why? Convertibles would be a good pick for these investors because of their principal protection features, but also because they could help grow their investments at a faster pace than simple bonds. Simply put, there's far greater potential upside. Using the Bank of America Merrill Lynch Convertible Bond (V0A0) index as an example, convertibles have beaten corporate and government debt, the Standard & Poor's 500, and the high yield indexes over the period of 1973–2012.

Convertibles as an Asset Class

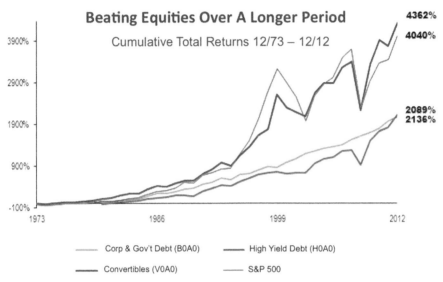

Beating Equities Over A Longer Period

Cumulative Total Returns 12/73 – 12/12

4362%
4040%
2089%
2136%

3900%
2900%
1900%
900%
-100%

1973   1986   1999   2012

——— Corp & Gov't Debt (B0A0)   ——— High Yield Debt (H0A0)
——— Convertibles (V0A0)   ——— S&P 500

Convertibles are an asset class that has been utilized for over 150 years

Convertible Bond Index began in 1973. Please see descriptions of indexes in the appendix.

Protection for Stock Investors

By similar logic, convertibles are a good bet for investors who are attracted to the potential payoffs of riskier products, such as stocks. Who doesn't like the upside of stocks? You'd be hard-pressed to find an investor who doesn't want to partake in the magnificent runs that stocks can experience every so often. That crazy red line that goes up and down on the index charts can be exhilarating as often as it is devastating. Stocks have created wealth for many. You hear about them as often as you hear about lottery winners—local man makes good, buys Apple when everyone else thought he was a nut and the company was about to go under. We could go on ...

But there's simply more to consider. It would be negligent advising and investing practice to ignore the inevitable downside of the upside. As crash after crash has shown us, the market doesn't play favorites, and it can break you as quickly as it made you. Trying to pick winners is like gambling or playing the lottery—you can do all the research you'd like, but ultimately there are more forces at play than you can control. An important step to absolute-return investing with convertibles is accepting the precept that investing in stocks is gambling. You wouldn't take your life savings to Vegas, would you? Thought so.

Investing with the TRW index in mind means that you've got a different goal in mind than gambling with your money. You'd like to see reasonable, consistent returns over the long term, and you understand that the long term includes downswings as well as the ups. If this sounds like you, then this strategy may be a good fit.

Convertibles have several advantages over equities, and the big three appeal to investors who don't want to gamble.

First, convertibles have favorable leverage. What this means is that a convertible bond will typically *rise* more than it will *fall* on equal movements of the underlying common stock. That means that even if a stock is on a downward trend, the convertible product attached to that stock still stands a good chance of turning a profit. This was certainly the case with the AOL Time Warner bond we discussed in the earlier chapters.

Second, convertibles have a higher-ranking claim on the

company's assets in the event of default or bankruptcy. This means that, as a convertible holder, you're in line before the legions of disappointed shareholders clamoring for whatever piece of the pie (generally slim to none) they can take. Keep in mind that all bondholders, including straight debt holders and convertible-bond investors, must get back 100% of their principal in a bankruptcy or default, *before* common stockholders get back one penny of their investment.

Finally, convertibles have greater potential for current income. You invest to make money. Because convertibles generally pay higher income than their underlying stocks—when you consider the interest rates as well as the yield to the next put option that you can exercise—they make a wonderful fit for investors who are looking to raise the value of their portfolio in incremental, conservative amounts. The pie keeps getting larger with convertibles, without as many market sharks taking bites out along the way.

Over time, we believe the numbers speak for themselves. Take, for example, a million dollars "invested" across the TRW index at the end of 1999 and held through the end of 2012. (Remember: you can't invest in any index, including TRW and the others shown in the following chart. The index serves as a proxy for "investing in convertibles under an absolute-return-seeking strategy.") If we were to crunch the numbers and look back on that period of time, there'd be times when equities as well as the convertibles index itself outperformed TRW. But, if you were to fast-forward to the endgame, you'd see a remarkable figure: in December 2012, that same portfolio invested on the TRW index would be worth almost $2.8 million, an advantage over the S&P of well over $1.5 million! Indeed, the S&P barely grew at all.

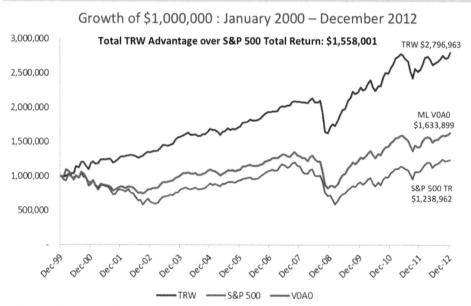

Investing with Convertibles – Performance vs Equities

Growth of $1,000,000 : January 2000 – December 2012

Total TRW Advantage over S&P 500 Total Return: $1,558,001

TRW $2,796,963

ML V0A0 $1,633,899

S&P 500 TR $1,238,962

Please see descriptions of indexes in the appendix. All numbers are approximate.

Clearly, it doesn't pay to ignore safer strategies like convertibles in favor of more volatile equities for a few reasons, not the least of which is that, no matter what the result is financially—even if you broke even with the S&P—you'd have done it in a way that exposed you to much, much more risk and volatility. Especially if you've got a family to support, or if you're looking towards using your portfolio to fund your retirement, it's crucial that you not take on too much risk.

Think about it: even if the end results are the same once, that doesn't necessarily mean that you'll roll the dice equivalently each time. An equity investor can see dramatic gains, but also horrible losses. We believe a limited risk investment strategy-based portfolio is much less likely to have the detrimental outcome, simply based on the safeguards in place when you invest with long-only convertible bonds and notes. Your principal is protected, cushioning your initial investment, and your gains have been made in a more safeguarded progression. It's a win-win that beats the win-lose rollercoaster ride.

The rollercoaster metaphor couldn't be more apt when it comes to investing in high-dividend stocks. Even if investors have thoroughly explored their risk tolerance with their advisors, it's hard to consider risk of loss objectively, when the focus is directed more at returns, especially during a bull market. Investors, ever optimistic, are prone to overemphasize the upward climb of the rollercoaster in their minds, not fully willing to consider the likelihood of a precipitous drop. They don't want to know about the dark side of volatility, or find out what you see when you look deeper, such as the maximum drawdown statistic for any given fund or product.

The maximum drawdown is the difference between the high point to the low point (or peak to trough). You can see these easily drawn out in red ink all over the pages of your favorite financial publication or in charts and graphs on the news. But those aren't what matter to any given investor. What should matter is the point where that individual investor put money in and lost it—if they bought high and sold low, ultimately losing more than an investor who bought low and sold lower, or someone who fell in between.

Recall my earlier story about my father. He fell victim to a severe and prolonged drawdown on what investors generally consider a very successful mutual fund: Fidelity Magellan. While few can dispute its long-term success, that doesn't mean that it hasn't had magnificently horrible drawdowns in the past. When markets and other circumstances conspire to create a drawdown, there's nothing the rookie investor can do to prepare for that spectacular failure. For instance, in 1973 (around the time my dad invested), an oil crisis contributed to an atmosphere of overall economic crisis in the United States. This caused Fidelity Magellan to slip in value from $34.26 per share to $10.37 per share, a free fall of almost 70% in twenty-one months! By the end of 1974, it had recovered just slightly, to $11.59 per share. Even by the end of the following year, in a strong rally, it had only increased a few dollars more. Today, Fidelity Magellan has recouped those losses, but most of those early investors—including my own father—didn't stick with it (who could blame them?). Even sadder, some simply didn't live long enough to get their money back.

Drawdowns happen to stocks and stock mutual funds, and they can be severe. But this is not what the court of popular opinion would have you believe. Open any financial website or tune in to any popular financial television or radio show and you're likely to find experts who are singing the siren song of investing in high-dividend stocks. "Don't be like your parents!" they caution, wagging their fingers. "They could have made so much more money if they had just invested in stocks. Are you just going to use a savings account for the rest of your life? A piggy bank? Come play with the big kids!"

It's tempting. I get it. Trumpeting the praises of high-dividend stocks isn't new, although sometimes you'll have a break from it after a spectacular crash, like the one in 2008. The immediate post-2008 period seemed to signal a new age of austerity and caution for investors and (allegedly) Wall Street and financial institutions. It lasted a New York minute or two, and, as so often happens in history, people forget or choose to ignore reality. They jump in again with the blindfold on.

As it turns out, shifting some of your assets from bonds to dividend-paying stocks isn't all bad. I'm not saying it's terrible advice. But the smart investor should know that there are two sides to every coin—and the advice that would have you shift your asset allocation this way has good and bad ideas wrapped up in it. It's a two-sided situation, presided over by the devil and angel on your shoulder. As a thought experiment, we should give in to both for a moment and listen to both sides of the argument.

The argument in favor of dividend-paying stocks has some merit to it. Stocks seem to be cheaper than bonds by most standards of measurement, and their potential for earning is high. Bonds, of course, are slow to grow and tied to interest rates—meaning they aren't going to pay very much at the present moment.

This argument is not new. Conventional wisdom has been, for the longest time, that stocks are ultimately going to return more than bonds and other products. Since they carry with them a higher degree of risk, the idea has been that they should also have a greater upside, as well. As the 2008 market crash recently showed us, that is definitely not always the case.

Now, let's consider the argument against a dividend stock

strategy. It's not complicated, and can be summed up in one word: **risk**. In the August 27, 2012, issue of *Barron's*, writer Jacqueline Doherty sums up the risk inherent in investing in high-dividend stocks very well. Her article, which quotes from research by Vadim Zlotnikov, chief market strategist at AllianceBernstein, is also attuned to the lessons that we should have learned in the last market crash after the housing bubble burst. She writes, "Winning trades rarely stay winning indefinitely. ... 'The risk of owning these [dividend-paying] stocks is that they are 20% to 25% overvalued,' and any increase in inflation or bond yields could cause them to tumble."

That doesn't sound so far-fetched after 2008, does it?

For some investors, risk is defined differently. Investors who are still attracted to dividend-paying stocks may define risk as losing purchasing power over time. Those investors fear a rise in stocks and not participating in that. This would mean missing out on an opportunity for massive gains. For other investors, however, risk is defined in the more traditional sense—the risk that one's capital will be lost, either gone forever or, just as bad, gone at the very moment that capital is needed. These investors are especially worried about their principal investment, as they should be.

In either case, convertible bonds are an option that should not be ignored. They are one of the few investments that not only can produce returns but can also help investors manage their risk exposure. As we've stated before, in the vast majority of the cases that we've documented and that we would advocate for future investment, convertibles will produce returns while protecting an investor's principal. And, just because there is risk management going on behind the scenes doesn't mean that you won't be able to partake in the upside if you invest in convertibles—if the underlying stock skyrockets, you'll still be able to take some advantage of that.

Finally, investing in convertibles relies far less on *market timing* than does investing in high-dividend paying stocks. We've gone over the dangers of market timing, but just to recap, very bluntly—it's nearly impossible to gain an advantage in any consistent way. Leave the gambling to the gamblers, and get to making smart investments for yourself.

A unique feature of investing in convertible bonds using the TRW strategy is that, in a way, it can accomplish "market timing" for you. In bull stock markets, convertibles take on many of the attributes of stocks, going up with the market. But in bear markets, convertibles deploying the TRW strategy take on much of the characteristics of straight fixed income, paying interest and protecting your principal.

Convertibles shouldn't be lumped in with other bonds, either, when comparing them to higher-dividend products. If a person points out that bonds are paying out absolutely nothing these days when compared to high-dividend stocks, you should point out to them that bonds and convertible bonds are apples and oranges.

While it's true that the current market environment has wreaked havoc on products that depend on interest rates, it's not true that this brutally challenging market has completely stripped convertibles of their finer points. Convertibles are still attractive when compared to the alternatives. They've managed to hold onto much of their luster, even in this challenging economic time. Take, for example, the well-known dot-com survivor, eBay. eBay is the Internet's premier auctioneer, and they recently raised several billion in capital at historically low rates through bond offerings. Of that capital, $250 million was at 0.7% for three years. That is absolutely remarkable! Can you imagine taking out a loan that size and only paying your creditors 0.7% interest on it for three years?

When comparing that to a convertible, where that bond offering starts to lose ground is when you look at the conversion price and premium. Unlike a convertible bond, there is no upside. eBay stock, which is at $49.09 a share as of this writing in September of 2012, could go up to $1,000.00 a share—and the bondholder wouldn't see a dime of that upside.

eBay and other companies might be getting free money from their investors, but that doesn't mean that you have to lose out entirely. If you invest with convertibles, you can still retain much of the upside of rising stock prices—even in a challenging market environment like the one we face today.

Investors who seek to reduce their exposure to stocks while at the same time keeping some of the upside, as convertibles allow them to do, will often find the best of both worlds when they use convertibles as part of the TRW index strategy.

Convertibles for Retirees

Many times, the goal of long-term investors is to make sure they're provided for in, well, the "long term!" Their time horizon is long, but that doesn't mean that they're going to bury their head in the sand and avoid looking at the future. Far from it: They're counting down the years, months, even days until they can drive home from the retirement dinner the firm has thrown for them and sleep soundly, knowing that in the morning, it will be time for the rest of their lives to start. These people have worked hard all of their lives, and now they want to sit back and let their hard-earned money do some of the heavy lifting for them.

For these investors, convertibles should represent a crucial component of a well-balanced retirement portfolio. Because of the lower-risk, principal-protected profile of the convertible bond, convertibles can represent the type of conservative investment needed to buttress the portfolio of someone on a fixed income. Conversely, in times of smooth sailing, convertibles continue to offer positive returns, keeping with the strategy of positive absolute returns across all market cycles. This is exactly the sort of investment that someone on a fixed income should really be looking hard at—it's easier for someone with working years ahead of them to justify waiting on the bull market to come along and help them recoup some of their losses, but if you're on a fixed income, your investments aren't likely to recover in time. What's worse, if your portfolio is too exposed to risk, you could end up outliving your money. And that extra worry and uncertainty is not something you signed up for when you decided it was time to finally take a break.

The first thing that happens when people start to ask questions about life after retirement is that investors will go to their financial advisor and ask for a hard and fast figure, based on what they have in the coffers at that moment, that they can expect to draw each year from their retirement fund. Retirees are especially concerned, and rightfully so, about outliving their money, and want to make sure that doesn't happen to them.

I've heard over the years anything from 3% to 6%, as a rule of thumb, but I've found that the average investment advisor seems to say that an annual withdrawal of 5% is a good number. By "good" I mean a number that won't invade principal. Of course, every retiree's expenses are different and every retirement account is different, but for the purposes of this example, we'll use 5%.

So let's say that as of December 31, 1999, our retirees—we'll call them Mr. and Mrs. Conservative—have $1 million in the bank. Mr. and Mrs. Conservative have done well for themselves! Let's say they got there through hard work and patience, and didn't just experience a giant windfall courtesy of the lottery or something similar. Chances are, the Conservative family is probably looking for a retirement strategy that mirrors their lifelong philosophy, and they truly value their portfolio. To them, this money is more than just a figure on a brokerage statement. It represents the life that they hope to lead after retirement, the travel and enjoyment they can experience now that they have time. This fund also needs to provide a financial safety net for Mr. and Mrs. Conservative in the case of accident or illness. The Conservatives' portfolio may need to pay for nursing home and other healthcare costs, as the couple ages. And, like many retirees, Mr. and Mrs. Conservative would love to leave a little something for their children and grandchildren. More than anything, these funds need to keep Mr. and Mrs. Conservative financially independent into old age.

So hypothetically, let's invest Mr. and Mrs. Conservative's money using two different strategies and see how those figures come out. The chart below tells the tale. The first strategy is, of course, exemplified by the TRW index. In this version, Mr. and Mrs. Conservative have tasked their like-minded advisor with investing in long-only convertibles with short-term liquidity dates built in and a proven record of performance.

Now, let's pretend that Mr. and Mrs. Conservative go to a different, more aggressive advisor, who convinces them to invest in other products, and is measuring their return by the Standard & Poor's 500 index.

Investing with Convertibles – Growth of $1M Invested on December 31, 1999

	TRW				S&P 500 Total Return		
Year	% Inc (Dec)	Balance	Annual 5% Withdrawal	Year	% Inc (Dec)	Balance	Annual 5% Withdrawal
2000	18.1%	1,180,842	59,042	2000	-9.1%	909,000	45,450
2001	8.1%	1,212,150	60,607	2001	-11.9%	760,874	38,044
2002	5.1%	1,210,295	60,515	2002	-22.1%	563,085	28,154
2003	17.3%	1,348,137	67,407	2003	28.7%	688,349	34,417
2004	7.4%	1,374,867	68,743	2004	10.9%	725,079	36,254
2005	2.0%	1,332,324	66,616	2005	4.9%	722,646	36,132
2006	12.0%	1,418,168	70,908	2006	15.8%	794,983	39,749
2007	7.8%	1,452,220	72,611	2007	5.5%	796,696	39,835
2008	-17.7%	1,134,827	56,741	2008	-37.0%	476,823	23,841
2009	34.0%	1,444,101	72,205	2009	26.5%	572,841	28,642
2010	12.1%	1,538,367	76,918	2010	15.1%	626,155	31,308
2011	-1.1%	1,445,132	72,257	2011	2.1%	607,398	30,370
2012	10.1%	1,511,370	75,568	2012	16.0%	669,353	33,468

Total Return: 51.1%   Total Return: (33.1)%

Total return is net of annual withdrawal. Numbers shown above are hypothetical. Total return includes the impact of withdrawals. Please see descriptions of indexes in the appendix. All numbers are approximate.

Let's compare the two options:

In 2000, 2001, and 2002, the markets declined dramatically. The S&P went down 9.10%, 11.89%, and 22.10%, respectively. For a working investor, that would represent a heck of a set-back—they'll need to wait a couple of years for their investments to bounce back, and they can probably count on tacking another couple of years onto their target retirement date while they're at it, unless they could somehow magically freeze all their spending needs and sell off some luxury cars in the process. But for someone like the Conservatives who just began their retirement adventure? You're talking the beginning of a catastrophe.

Each year of that bear market, Mr. and Mrs. Conservative's more aggressive account is going to dwindle—not just from the fluctuations of the market, but from their planned 5% withdrawals. And as the size of the account dwindles, so does the amount that Mr. and Mrs. Conservative can safely withdraw using the 5% figure. So, in each of those years, the value of their portfolio under a stock-based strategy declined to $909,000 in 2000, $760,874 in 2001, and $563,085 in 2002. Already, they're down to almost *half* of what they had invested only three short years before. And the withdrawals are equally depressing: The first year, Mr. and Mrs. Conservative only have $45,450 to live on. Okay, maybe they can make that work. The second year though, they only have $38,044. And the third year, all the way down to $28,154.

Consider, however, the hypothetical investment in convertible bonds using the limited risk investment strategy represented by the TRW index. In 2000, this portfolio actually saw an increase of just over 18%, bringing the balance above the starting point—$1.18 million. And that's in a bear market. So right off the bat, the Conservatives were able to withdraw 5% of that, a comfortable $59,042 to live on for the year. In 2001, the increase was more modest: 8%, bringing the balance up to over $1.2 million. That year, they could withdraw a little more, $60,607, after the additional influx of cash from the increase in portfolio value. The third year, Mr. and Mrs. Conservative were still able to cover (just about) their planned withdrawal, a lot better than the S&P 500 alternative-style investing plan would have treated them.

They were still able to withdraw $60,515 (as 5% of the total) that year, whereas under their more aggressive strategy, they would not have been able to withdraw half that much. The intervening years will see many ups and downs as well, as we know from living through those and other markets. In 2008, which was far and away the worst market environment seen in this hypothetical example, we see that the S&P went down a whopping 37%. By that time, the aggressive portfolio was down to less than half its original value: $476,823. The Conservatives could only withdraw $23,841 to live on that year. Mr. and Mrs. Conservative, following the TRW index, took a hit, too. The portfolio went down 17.7% but still stayed over the initial value—and they were able to withdraw $56,741.

If we follow these hypothetical figures to their ends, the "winner" is clear: a 51% return net of withdrawals over the course of twelve years for Mr. and Mrs. Conservative using the TRW strategy, and a total loss of 33% for Mr. and Mrs. Conservative if they invested following the S&P. The balance of the second portfolio is down to two-thirds whereas the first has actually *grown*.

Obviously, this represents a much safer, much more stable way for retirees to live—knowing that their investments are going to continue to work and that they'll not only be able to make withdrawals each year but also watch their investment *grow* at the same time.

Savvy retirees may like to compare some other products—maybe other conservative, fixed-income products such as bonds. Common investment advice may steer you to repositioning some of your assets such that the closer you get to retirement age, the greater the presence of bonds in your portfolio—especially if you participate in a target retirement date fund. We've talked a bit about the difference between straight bonds and convertible bonds, and you probably know where we stand on our preference! But don't take our word for it—just look at the quantifiable evidence that investing in convertibles using this strategy will outpace straight bonds.

The implication is clear: for investors with a long-term investment horizon and who have the discipline and staying power to keep their funds in one place, the limited-risk investment strategy using the TRW index is the way to go.

12

What About Convertible Arbitrage?

"Convertible arbitrage," is a term you may have heard about. What is it? What most people mean when they use this term is the practice of buying convertible securities while simultaneously selling short a certain amount of the same company's underlying shares.

While the convertible arbitrage crowd impacts the convertible bond market, we do not recommend convertible arbitrage as a strategy for most individual investors. It's certainly not something to take on by yourself. But here is an explanation for the curious.

The period from the mid-1990s to the onset of the financial crisis in 2007 was, by and large, the golden era of the strategy of convertible arbitrage, or "convert arb" for short. Convert arb is a strategy dominated by hedge funds. Some hedge-fund managers got impossibly rich during this period, some led by Ken Griffin, whose beginnings trading convertibles from his Harvard dorm room in the 1980s are legendary in the industry.

The idea of convert arb is to create a portfolio that will not react to small moves in the underlying stock but that will turn profits on large ones. Small upward moves in the underlying stock, for instance, create losses on the short stock position (or "hedge") that will be offset by gains in the market value of the convertible bonds. In down markets, the gains on the short stock make up for declines in the convertibles.

The theory behind the strategy is that large moves by the stock, in either direction, will typically result in profits. This is because with most convertible arbitrage positions, the portfolio manager or trader does not sell short the full amount of stock controlled by the convertible bond. Since convertibles typically move up and down at a slower rate than the underlying stock, it stands to reason that a neutral hedge would involve selling less than all the shares controlled.

Consider the extreme cases. When a stock has performed poorly—as in AOL Time Warner—the convertible bond becomes insensitive to moves in the stock. It trades instead like a bond, a yield instrument. The other extreme is the Home Depot story, where the stock goes far above the conversion price and turns the convertible into a nearly perfect substitute for the shares.

In the AOL Time Warner case, if you're a convertible-arbitrage type, you would end up with no shares short against your bonds. With Home Depot, you'd end up shorting all the shares your bond controlled. Remember, you're trying to keep a neutral position. In the middle, you'd have some kind of neutral hedge—somewhere between half and two-thirds of the underlying stock, on average.

So let's think about what happens when the stock makes a big move and the convertible does what it's supposed to do. On the downside, it falls to a level where it can trade just as a plain bond, and then it stops falling. This might be 10%-20% of the original price, sometimes more, sometimes less. But it's a lot less than the kind of fall the stock might take.   So with a decent short position as an initial hedge—even if it's a lot less than the full amount of shares the bond controls—there's terrific opportunity for profit.

On the upside, because you've left between a third and a half of the shares you control unhedged, there's also opportunity to make plenty of money if you're a convertible arbitrageur.

The "golden age" of convertible arbitrage saw big profits when stocks moved aggressively higher (in the mid-to-late 1990s) and lower (in the early 2000s). Indeed, the unwinding of the dot-com era was a great boon to convertible arbitrageurs who were able to identify companies that would stay in business (and pay off their convertible bonds at face value) even as their stocks lost 80%-90% of their value.

But when the moves are small, it gets tricky. This is especially because convertibles, as we've seen, trade at a premium to the underlying shares. When the shares move up gradually over time—as they often do—the premium slowly dissipates. This doesn't really hurt investors who just buy the convertibles as a long-only, buy-and-hold position, because the gains in the stock push the convertible to higher prices. But it does hurt convertible arbitrageurs, because the relatively small gains in the convertible bond get eaten up by losses in the short stock.

This is especially a problem because the convertible arbitrage strategy often depends on leverage. Portfolio managers typically borrow between one and three times their capital to buy additional convertible bonds and hedge them. When stocks creep higher and convertibles leak premium, positions that would generate acceptable profits for unhedged investors can result not only in losses but also in losses magnified by leverage. Most of the investors in convertible arbitrage funds are told they are buying a market-neutral strategy. When losses come about—and they do, in a variety of scenarios including the one we just described—these investors, typically fast-money accounts like funds of hedge funds, tend to pull out quickly. Thus modest losses can quickly accelerate, again because of leverage.

Longer-term, unhedged investors, such as those following an absolute-return-oriented strategy as represented by the TRW Index, repeatedly benefit from the playing out of this cycle. They are able to buy convertibles from liquidating hedge funds and hold them without concern about short-term mark-to-market issues. For this reason, in spite of all the riches convertible arbitrage funds have generated for certain individuals, the asset class of convertible bonds is far better suited to long-term buy-and-hold unhedged investors.

The financial crisis of 2008 drastically shifted the balance of power away from hedge funds and toward long-only investors. In the early months of 2008, a huge amount—around $30 billion—of new convertible securities were issued by the financial services industry, just months ahead of the meltdown. Most of these were bought by hedge funds, which at the time owned about 75% of the domestic convertible bond market.

After Lehman Brothers (one of the firms that did a multi-billion-dollar convertible issue early in 2008) went bankrupt, the government for a short time, and without much notice, prohibited the short sale of about nine hundred financial stocks. This resulted in the unplanned consequence of the convertible arb folks' short positions becoming illegal overnight. This made it impossible for hedge funds to trade their positions in those new convertibles and destroyed their value, leading directly to the liquidation or shrinkage of most convertible hedge funds. They still have not come close to recovering and now control only about half as much of the market as they did before the meltdown.

The lesser prominence of hedge funds in the convertible market has both positive and negative implications for longer-term convertible investors. The good side is that convertible holders are less prone to the market fluctuations brought on by leveraged hedge funds. The negative is that hedge funds can be an important source of ongoing liquidity, because they are constantly trading for smaller gains than buy-and-hold types. While it's unclear whether the market is better or worse off with hedge funds playing a smaller role, there's little doubt that the convertible asset class is best suited to investors who don't need to worry about day-to-day price changes.

13

Convertible Stories:
Baxter, Our 20th Anniversary Convertible (2011)

Clients and prospects have been telling us for over twenty years that they haven't heard of convertible bonds before, and sometimes people guess that they must be new. In reality, convertibles have been around for over a hundred years, and on our walls hang some of the certificates to prove it. In many cases, the bonds still have the coupons attached. In former times, one had to clip off the coupon to get the interest, and we still use the term "coupon" to refer to bond interest rates and payments today.

If you've visited our Wellesley office, you might have noticed the framed, original convertible bonds (most of them quite old) that we have hanging on our walls. We thought it would be interesting to research one—Baxter Laboratories—and share the story with you.

Baxter Laboratories was founded in 1931 as the first manufacturer and distributor of intravenous (IV) solutions. During its first few years of operation, the company distributed products that were manufactured in a Los Angeles facility owned by Dr. Don Baxter until it opened a more central manufacturing facility in Glenville, Illinois, in 1933.

The fledgling company prospered and in 1935, Dr. Ralph Falk purchased Dr. Baxter's interest in the firm and organized a research and development function to continue the firm's advances in medical technology. In 1939, Baxter Laboratories introduced the Transfuso-Vac container, which allowed blood storage for up to twenty-one days, making blood banking possible.

Continuing into the 1940s, Baxter Laboratories introduced other medical advances and in 1945, William B. Graham, a young patent lawyer, joined the company and eventually succeeded Dr. Falk as CEO. Under Mr. Graham's leadership, the firm was credited with one of the most exceptional growth records in American industry. It is Mr. Graham's signature that appears on the Baxter convertible bond we have hanging in our office.

In 1956, based on a kidney dialysis invention by Dr. Willem Kolff, which he constructed with orange juice cans and a washing machine, Baxter engineers introduced the first commercially built artificial kidney. This is just one example of the firm's lengthy list of medical solutions that have contributed to saving countless lives. Over the next several decades, Baxter Laboratories experienced tremendous growth and expanded internationally.

Baxter International Inc. (NYSE: BAX) is now a global leader in the healthcare industry, developing and marketing medical products and pharmaceuticals that help people with a variety of chronic and severe medical illnesses. In 2012, the company had over fifty thousand employees and sales of $14.2 billion.

We named the Baxter convertible bond our 20th Year Anniversary Convertible because it matured in 1991, the year Wellesley Investment Advisors was founded.

14

When Interest Rates Rise

As you have learned in previous chapters, convertible bonds provide the opportunity for investors to participate in the upside of equity markets while also offering potential downside protection. Because convertibles possess both equity and bond attributes, they are particularly useful in managing a portfolio's risk/return profile.

A common question many potential investors raise is, "What will happen to convertible bonds when the inevitable Fed tightening occurs and interest rates head upward again?"

Most investors know that historically, interest rate hikes have been devastating for almost all types of fixed income investments including Treasuries, corporate bonds, and municipal bonds. A convertible bond, however, is a hybrid investment that can be exchanged or converted into a specific number of shares of common stock.

What would happen to this investment vehicle when the Fed starts to tighten again?

In December 2009, *Barron's* magazine shed some light on what might happen to convertible bonds when interest rates start to rise again. In a *Barron's* cover story titled, "Even Better Than Bonds," *Barron's* stated,

> Investments like ... convertibles offer fat yields and a bulwark against rising rates or inflation. ... while hardly anything is as cheap or attractive as it was earlier this year ... converts offer appealing alternatives to increasingly unattractive bonds.

Barron's offered no empirical evidence that convertible bonds have performed well during past periods of raising interest rates. Wellesley Investment Advisors and the *Limited Risk Investor* obtained some research on how equities and convertibles have performed over the past fifty years, when the central bank tightened money supply. While the past is never a guarantee of future results, it is probably the best place to look for clues.

In the last fifty years, the Fed has tightened money policy 13 times. The average tightening period was fourteen months. During these periods of rising rates, the average rate increase was 4.5%. In all but two of these 13 tightening cycles, the S&P 500 increased. In fact, over the last fifty years, the S&P 500 has increased an average of 8.8% when the U.S. central bank raised interest rates. When we think about this, it makes sense. Why and when do governments raise interest rates? When the economy is expanding, and doing well. Further, in each of the periods when the S&P 500 fell against rising interest rates, the S&P declined by only 3.5% or less.

The data on the fallout (or lack thereof) from rate increases is logical and makes sense. Except during the Hoover administration of the 1930s, most Fed chairmen have realized that increasing interest rates while equity prices are falling is a dangerous policy. It can cause or prolong a recession or even drive the economy into a depression.

Our question, however, is this: exactly how have *convertibles* performed during these periods of rising interest rates? Bank of America Merrill Lynch supplied us with data regarding the Convertible Bond Index (V0A0) and how it performed, over the last twenty years, each time the Fed tightened monetary policy. The results are here:

Fed Tightening Cycles

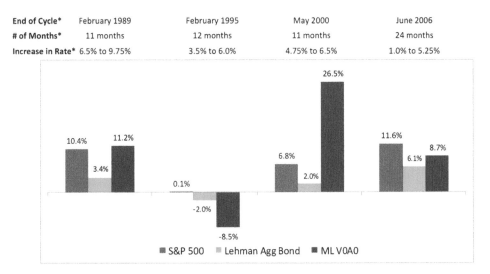

Performance of Key Indexes During Last 4 Fed Tightening Cycles

	February 1989	February 1995	May 2000	June 2006
End of Cycle*	11 months	12 months	11 months	24 months
# of Months*	11 months	12 months	11 months	24 months
Increase in Rate*	6.5% to 9.75%	3.5% to 6.0%	4.75% to 6.5%	1.0% to 5.25%

*Data provided by Deutsche Bank.
Please see descriptions of indexes in the appendix. All numbers are approximate.

It is interesting to note that in three out of the four most recent instances when the central bank tightened, convertible bonds went *up*. Twice, they actually rose more than the S&P 500 did. In the eleven-month Fed tightening cycle in 1999–2000, convertible bonds skyrocketed by over 26%, more than three times the gain in the S&P 500.

However, what happened in the February 1994–1995 cycle? Why did convertibles perform poorly during that Fed tightening period?

The answer to that is best explained by examining the nature of convertible bonds during that period. Before February 1995, most convertible bonds did not have *puts.*

As you know by now, convertible bonds with embedded puts allow the holder of a long-term convertible bond to force the company that issued the bond to buy it back at a predetermined price on prearranged dates, in accordance with a schedule in the bond's prospectus. The put feature of a convertible bond effectively turns a long-term bond into a short-term instrument. The bondholder has the option to shorten the holding period of the bond by forcing the issuer to buy the bond back at various dates before the bond's maturity.

During the twelve months of the 1994–1995 Fed tightening cycle, the S&P 500 stayed relatively flat, up only 0.13%. This was not enough to compensate for the fact that the average maturity of convertibles was very long-term during that period. Since 1995, the tremendous increase in the issuance of convertible bonds with puts has helped to mitigate Fed tightening and rate increases, as clearly evidenced by the next two interest-rate-increase cycles.

A senior convertible bond trader from Merrill Lynch said this about the '94–'95 Fed tightening:

> Converts got killed in '94 when underlying bond content was eroded with the rate spikes. The universe had longer duration back then in general, with many convert structures of twenty-plus years.

Today, most convertible-bond portfolios have much shorter durations because the majority of convertible bonds have either short-term maturities or puts. So, even when the Fed tightens from its historically low rate of 0.25%, convertible bonds may well follow their long-term pattern of rising along with equity prices.

15

Convertible Stories: Boston Chicken (1998)

Throughout the book, we've given you many successful examples of convertible bonds that our firm has invested in for our clients. We've also given you the caveat that there is no perfect strategy and there are no perfect outcomes. That doesn't mean, however, that you should throw caution to the wind. That's one of the lessons that we learned a long time ago from our experience with Boston Chicken.

Boston Chicken (now known as Boston Market) was a successful fast food franchise in the 1990s. Our firm purchased convertible bonds in Boston Chicken for a little over $28 on October 31, 1995. Like other companies we invest in, Boston Chicken had great numbers. Their stock was skyrocketing and everyone loved the company.

We sold it a little over two years later, on January 16, 1998—but not before we lost money on the deal.

News started to trickle out about some problems with Boston Chicken even as they were releasing numbers and earnings reports that painted a very rosy picture. Experts and the media had begun to question the veracity of those statements, and it became clear that Boston Chicken was engaged in some accounting practices that were at best highly questionable in their nature. This was before Enron or WorldCom, but strikes a very similar chord. Eventually, amid all of the questions and doubts surrounding these faulty accounting practices, the company went bankrupt.

There are three things to take from this—one is that getting back something is better than nothing, as the shareholders can attest. Another is that you should always be very careful when examining statements released by any company, and make sure you invest time and energy checking them out for yourself. But ultimately, you're not always going to know when you're receiving faulty information—even if you're the best advisor, investor, or money pro in the world. That brings us to the third lesson, which is the only one that you can actively do anything with (meaning, it's the only one of these three that's necessarily *under your control*): Always protect yourself by diversifying your portfolio.

The way to protect yourself in almost any convertible or other portfolio is to take small bites, never too much of any one thing, no matter how good things look. This is how you mitigate losses! We generally recommend putting no more than 4% of your portfolio in any bond. If you keep your exposures below 4%, you reduce the risk of being terribly hurt if things go south, and it's one of the only ways to protect yourself against situations like Boston Chicken. Of course, you need to do your due diligence, and we think it's best to buy bonds of companies whose financial statements are audited by one of the "Big 4" accounting firms. But sometimes, even if you've done everything right, you can still be victimized by a deceitful management team. So, only by diversifying your portfolio can you mitigate those losses.

No matter how wonderful a company looks or a how attractive a particular bond seems, there could always be something bubbling under the surface. Whether it's an unforeseen crisis, a seemingly wise decision that didn't work out, or fraud, there are no guarantees in life—or the market.

Diversifying the portfolio extends beyond your initial investment, too. When your portfolio's values shift, this obviously will result in each of your 4% allocations becoming less than 4% if the bond has declined, or more than 4% if the bond has done well. A prudent investor needs to review his or her portfolio periodically to "rebalance," often trimming back positions that have risen in value, before they become too large a component of the whole. It takes real discipline to do this, especially when the result is that you need to cut back on your holdings of your "winners." But that's what investors need to do if they want to reduce their overall risk.

16

Failing Grades, Revisited (2011)

In a 2007 edition of the *Limited Risk Investor,* our convertible bond newsletter, we wrote about the failure of the three major credit rating agencies (Standard & Poor's, Moody's, and Fitch) to properly rate corporate and government debt. We, along with many others, have noted the absolute inability of these agencies to do their jobs and appropriately rate sub-prime debt. All three rating agencies gave sub-prime debt pools their highest rating of AAA. Furthermore, the malfunction in rating sub-prime debt was nothing new to these agencies. They have performed miserably in the area of rating numerous municipal and corporate bonds. Another notorious example was their failure to downgrade companies like Enron until the company was on the brink of bankruptcy.

We attribute these serious shortcomings on the part of these agencies in part to what we call the "Arthur Andersen Effect." Like big CPA audit firms, the Big 3 rating agencies are paid by the companies they rate, rather than by investors who use their ratings. Smaller rating agencies, like Egan-Jones, which are retained by the investors who use them, have often issued much more accurate ratings than the Big 3 rating agencies.

Since we wrote our article in 2007, Henry Waxman, chairman of the House Oversight and Government Reform Committee stated, "The story of the credit rating agencies is a story of colossal failure." Waxman and others blame the rating agencies and federal regulators for putting the entire financial system at risk and betraying the public's trust.

Andrew Taylor, from the Associated Press, stated executives of the rating agencies were "well aware that there was little basis for giving AAA ratings to thousands of increasingly complex mortgage-related securities, but the companies often vouched for them anyway."

Have the rating agencies improved their performance since the disasters of pre-2009? Not according to (then) New York Attorney General Andrew Cuomo, who issued subpoenas to the three major credit rating agencies.

The following is an excerpt in the *Washington Post* describing an October 2008 posting from the oversight committee, while Waxman was laying into the rating agencies. Waxman is quoting anonymous executives from the rating agencies in documents his committee obtained: "'We sold our soul to the devil,' one ratings agency employee said. 'It could be structured by cows and we'd rate it,' said another. The story of the credit rating agencies is a story of a colossal failure," Waxman concluded.

We have wondered if any changes have been made after all that inquiry and outcry. Have the rating agencies changed their ratings systems? Has anything changed? We do not think so, and this is especially so with respect to their rating of convertible bonds, something we are able to observe daily. In 2010, top executives appeared before Congress again and were interrogated by Senator Carl Levin, whose opening statement included the following:

> For a hundred years, Main Street investors trusted U.S. credit rating agencies to guide them toward safe investments. Even sophisticated investors like pension funds, municipalities, insurance companies, and university endowments, have relied on credit ratings to protect them.
>
> But now, that trust has been broken. We used as case histories the two biggest credit rating agencies in the United States, Moody's and Standard & Poor's, and the ratings they gave to the key financial instruments that fueled the financial crisis—residential mortgage backed securities, or RMBS, and collateralized debt obligations, or CDOs. The Subcommittee investigation found that those credit rating agencies allowed Wall Street to impact their analysis, their independence, and their reputation for reliability. And they did it for the money.

While we always consider credit agency ratings of bonds, we have never relied solely on them. This is primarily because we have never found them to be sufficiently accurate and have noticed what appears to be a heavy bias toward larger capitalized companies who in turn pay high fees to the rating agencies.

If there is such a divergence between our fundamental analysis and those of the big rating agencies, why do so many institutions still rely on them? There are a few reasons. First, many institutions, like insurance companies, have rules that require them to purchase only "investment grade" bonds as rated by one of the major credit agencies. Hence, they really have no alternative. Another reason is many investors and advisors do not have the knowledge, time, or expertise to do an in-depth independent credit analysis. They rely solely on the credit agencies, for lack of any viable alternative. Yet another reason is that money managers can take cover in the rating agencies' work—if the bonds go bad, they have someone else to blame. Lastly, and somewhat remarkably, many investors do not realize the poor quality of ratings many of the agencies have produced over the years.

At Wellesley Investment Advisors, Inc., our investment team is comprised of CPAs and MBAs. We will look at the work of the rating agencies, but we will never rely solely on them. Instead, we perform independent credit analysis on every bond we buy and own. An important risk to consider when investing in bonds is default risk. By not putting all our faith in official ratings and doing our own direct analysis, we try to mitigate default risk as much as possible.

17 ———————————————

Convertible Stories:
Reebok (2003)

Reebok International (NYSE: RBK) designs, develops, and markets fitness and casual footwear and apparel products. This Stoughton, Massachusetts, company also designs and markets its products under other brand names such as Rockport, Ralph Lauren and Polo footwear, and Greg Norman brand athletic equipment. Although manufacturing such a variety of products under so many brand names can increase costs, Reebok has integrated operations and is sharing key technology platforms between its brands to reduce the cost of manufacturing different brands of products.

Back in 2002, the company's revenue rose 4.5% from the prior year, while net earnings leaped 23%. Reebok was receiving a favorable response to its NBA and NFL products, with endorsements from athletes from both arenas. In 2003, sales and earnings were up 9% and 8%, respectively, over the same period in 2002. Value Line estimated that the stock would shine in the years ahead with increases of about 45% over the next three years. However, despite all the attraction of Reebok, it was volatile.

Instead we purchased Reebok's convertible bond around March 1, 2002. On March 13, 2003, RBK's common stock closed at $31.70, an increase of 17.6% from the point of purchase. The investment grade convertible, 4.5% convertible bond due 2021, gained about 8.52% plus paid interest for a total return of 13.83%, during the same period. That's almost 80% of the gain of the common stock but with substantially less risk. The RBK convertible provided conservative investors with a steady stream of income for the life of the bond and had the additional benefit of a put. While holding this bond, investors had the option to force Reebok to repurchase the bond on March 1, 2008, for $1,021.25 if things didn't go so well.

Some convertible stories can be told as home runs—where the stock goes to a multiple of its initial price and the convertible comes along for a good portion of the ride. Others are strikeouts and in some ways are even more compelling, as they show that even on stocks that lose a significant portion of their value, convertibles can provide acceptable returns from income and the return of principal.

Then there are cases like Reebok—companies with exciting stories where the stock ends up performing respectably but not sensationally. In these instances, the convertible will typically generate modest positive absolute returns from some mix of coupon income and capital appreciation. These instances may not be flashy but they do represent a significant percentage of the outcomes.

18

Outrunning the Bear

We've talked about the unfortunate truth that all investors are at the mercy of market cycles to some extent—some certainly more than others, based on how their asset allocation looks. My grandfather and my father, both of whom saw their net worth that had been built up over years of hard work evaporate in bear markets, were powerless against these cycles.

These types of fickle, largely unpredictable downturns of the market are precisely what steered the development of the TRW index and strategy, and convertibles are the essence of that. This strategy is built with the following idea in mind: if you don't lose money (or don't lose much money) in a bear market (typically, a 20% or greater decline in market values), you don't need to make as much money in the bull market to accomplish favorable returns for full market cycles. If you tangle with the unfeeling bear too much, you're then dependent upon the unpredictable bull to drag you back out of the downward spiral your assets are stuck in.

Naysayers of the strategy might promise that they can time the market or take advantage of the inevitable bull market environment that comes along. While it's true that a complete market cycle does include a bull market by definition, it's not truthful to claim that you can absolutely know when that bull is going to happen, or even how many times it's going to happen. Again and again, investors mis-time the markets.

A Chicken in Every Pot, A Bear (or More) in Every Decade

In my own research, for example, I went back 120 years to look and see how many bear markets versus how many bull markets you could find per decade, according to data from the Dow Jones Industrial Average. These numbers are approximate, but they do paint a clear picture of the number of bear markets that investors have encountered each decade. (I did not use the Standard & Poor's 500, by the way, because the S&P 500 index did not come into existence until the 1950s.)

I had assumed that a bear market happened at least once every decade. But as I got further into my research, I found some facts that shocked me. *Most* decades, it turns out, had either two or three bear markets. Please see the chart on the following page. I know you've seen it before, but some things are worth repeating.

Every decade has had at least one (the 1920s, 1940s, 1950s, and 1990s only had one each, for example), but it's typical, going back for that amount of time, to see two or three. And even in decades where there was only one bear all by its lonesome, its bite was fierce: The 1920s, obviously, saw a 89% decline in their single bear market. Even worse, after the sole bear market of the decade of the 1920s, it took investors until the **1950s**—twenty-five years!—just to break even. Even though no bear market since has been that severe, the numbers in recent downturns are no joke. The last two

Convertibles as an Asset Class

Year	Number of Bear Markets	Percent Decline in DJIA
1900s	3	46%, 49%, 27%
1910s	3	24%, 40%, 47%
1920s	1	89%
1930s	3	23%, 49%, 41%
1940s	1	24%
1950s	1	19%*
1960s	3	27%, 26%, 36%
1970s	2	45%, 27%
1980s	2	24%, 36%
1990s	1	21%
2000s	2	38%, 53%

*Since the S&P 500 did have a 22% decline in 1957 many investment professionals consider the decade to have had a (single) bear market.

bear markets we've been through (2000–2003 and 2007–2009) saw declines of 38% (2003) and 53% (2009) decline, respectively.

Getting Back to Even: Hard, and Not Good Enough

The math speaks for itself: if you have a net worth of a million dollars and it drops 50% to $500,000, you now will need a 100% gain just to get back to even. And while there are no guarantees in the market, it's not fiscally sound to depend upon a once-in-a-lifetime miracle to make up your lost net worth. And remember, even if that figure is made up for on the upswing, which it may not be in your own lifetime, you still haven't gained anything. You've simply gotten back to your starting point—after a lot of agony. If you're looking long-term and hoping to secure yourself and your family for retirement, for example, then you've definitely *lost ground*, even if you've made back your original investment.

So by following an absolute-return-oriented strategy in convertibles—or, basically, the TRW index, which looks to generate positive returns across *complete market cycles* (not just during a bull market)—we think you'll be one step ahead of the market. You should no longer have to try to time up and down markets, something almost no one can do. The previous chart may be the most important chart in this book. For if unpredictable and frequent bear markets didn't occur, convertible bonds deploying the TRW strategy would not be necessary. Because convertible bonds deploying the TRW strategy are a valuable asset class in persevering and protecting wealth, they are better suited to a long-term strategy.

How Long Is Long?

Tied in with all this are some misconceptions about investing that have to do with an investor's time horizon and risk. The common thinking is that if you have a long time over which to hold your stocks, the risk is worth it, because over long periods of time, stocks can outperform other assets. And certainly, in some cases, there are figures to back this up—even in our own example of a home run with convertibles, the Home Depot example, the stock outperformed the convertible products in that case.

But more conservative investors will still protest. They might bring up the fact that stocks are also incredibly risky—definitely more volatile than fixed-income products or convertible bonds (remember how in some of our examples, even when the stock of a company plummeted, you could still possibly see a positive return on your investment in convertibles?). Those who favor stocks might say that stocks that have performed well in the past will likely perform well in the future, or that if an investor has a long time horizon, as opposed to a short-term investment need, they would do well in stocks. Accordingly, their advice might be to make stocks a cornerstone of their portfolio. Moreover, many investment advisors often insist that a well-balanced portfolio *must* include stocks as a key component. "Don't worry," they may tell you, "Those volatile stocks aren't *all of your* portfolio. Just *some*." The definition of "some" depends on the investor—for *some* investors, "some" of their portfolio can represent hundreds of thousands of dollars, even more!

But, no matter what soothing words your advisor might whisper in your ear, the realities of the inevitable bear markets, in addition to other fluctuations and unforeseen circumstances (AOL Time Warner, anyone?) should still make you feel wary, and with good reason. It's difficult enough for investors to go around picking winners for their portfolio in the first place, but on top of that, you should think of what your time horizon actually means. If you are truly investing in the long term, you're likely investing with your retirement and your family's security in mind. What if you *do* invest largely in those risky stocks, and when the time comes, those stocks don't do as well? What if they not only underperform but also fall dramatically? You'll watch your retirement fund go down the drain.

In simple terms, it's a fallacy that your time horizon can accurately account for your risk tolerance (how much risk you're able to take on in your portfolio). The conventional wisdom says that the longer your time horizon, the more risk you can take on in your asset allocation, simply because you have time to absorb market fluctuations. Assuming you sit on your investments like a patient investor instead of yanking your money out every time the market flags, you'll do well over the long term, especially with stocks.

Or so they say.

But the whole story is more complicated than that, as is often the case. In reality, stocks can even be quite risky in the long run. It's a fact that returns *can* be lower than expected, even for several years in a row—and that can happen just as easily fifty years from now as it can five years from now. Stocks don't just stop becoming a risky proposition just because you've got time on your side. Obviously, this presents a problem if your stocks are on the downswing when you need to draw down on your portfolio, but it would also be a problem throughout the investment process— years of successive losses can have a devastating impact on the ending value of your portfolio, meaning that you might not be able to meet your financial goals. Even austerity measures might not help. We're talking serious business here: the possibility that, with your portfolio suffering, you'll outlive your money.

The current conventional wisdom has many loud promoters but leaves out one crucial component that must be considered. As an investor's time horizon lengthens, there are a greater number of possible outcomes for the value of their portfolio. Current events, market trends, unforeseen Act-of-God type circumstances can all come into play—and the longer an investment sits on the market, the more exposure there can be to these types of events. The widening ranges of end values for portfolios will, then, potentially also include severe actual underperformance when compared to the theoretical values that the investment strategy was based on. Projections are just that: projections. Reality is firm and final.

This is not meant to be alarmist. This isn't going to be the case for everyone who invests in the stock market, or who hangs onto stocks as part of their retirement portfolio. But the fact that this hypothetical can and does happen (we've seen how many bear markets can occur per decade) is worth careful consideration. This isn't so much an aberration to ignore as a likelihood to ponder. Avoiding losses in the first place, rather than worrying about making gains that you ultimately have no control over, is the cornerstone of the TRW index strategy.

19

Convertible Stories: Starwood (2004)

Starwood Hotels & Resorts Worldwide (NYSE: HOT) owns, operates, and franchises hotel properties under brand names for the upscale market including Sheraton, Westin, St. Regis and W. The company has more than 740 properties in over eighty countries with total rooms in excess of 224,000. The company's revenue and earnings derive primarily from hotel operations, which include the operation of the company's owned hotels, management and other fees earned from hotels that the company manages, pursuant to management contracts, and the receipt of franchise fees.

Despite net revenue rising slightly during 2003, net income fell 13%, when compared to the prior year, because of higher selling and administrative costs, as well as disposition and impairment charges. This earnings shortfall did not, however, deter investors from buying Starwood common stock. In fact, the stock price rose 47% during 2003 in the face of poor earnings, indicating investors' confidence in the company's long-term prospects. Analysts expected the company to rebound in 2004, with earnings per share expected to rise by 39%, and stock price target range of $40 to $65 in the upcoming three-to-five-year period.

In spite of all of the above, we felt Starwood's stock was not suitable for risk-averse investors. For investors looking to lower their exposure to the high level of risk in the common stock, we instead recommended the company's 3.5% convertible due in 2023 as an alternative. The relative volatility of the convertible (one indicator of risk) was half that of the common stock, and the convertible had a 1.2% current yield advantage over the common stock. The convertible displayed strong upside participation potential in the underlying stock and limited downside exposure. Furthermore, the convertibles were call-protected until May 23, 2006. Investors had the ability to shorten the maturity of the notes by forcing the company to repurchase them at par on May 16, 2006. The bonds were rated BB+ by Standard & Poor's (slightly below investment grade), and had a yield to the next put of slightly below 1%. We weren't buying because 1% was such a great yield—we were buying because we thought we had plenty of upside (unless we had made a huge error in judging the credit) with no downside.

You may wonder what we mean by the bonds being "call-protected." As long as an issuer cannot call (force you to sell back, typically at or around the issue price) a convertible bond, the holder has access to the underlying stock's upside potential. So call protection is a period of time during which investors stand to gain from a rise in the stock. Investors must be especially careful about the prices they pay for convertible bonds with little or no call protection, or risk having the bond called away at a loss. Essentially, call protection gives investors upside, while its expiration allows the issuer to force investors to choose between taking cash or stock in exchange for the convertible bond. Just because an issuer can call a convertible does not mean it will—but investors (and especially their advisors) must be mindful nonetheless.

Starwood might not quite have been a home run for investors, but it was a very profitable holding. We bought the bonds in March 2004 at slightly above 106. The bonds thus had only a slightly positive yield to the May 2006 put and call dates, and we were buying them with the hope of substantial equity gains. We got them. From March 2004 to May 2006, Starwood equity returned better than 90% including dividends. We sold the bonds in early May 2006 at about 148 just before the call date. Investors in the convertibles thus reaped a total gain of just under fifty points (forty-two in appreciation and the rest from income) or about 47%, thus participating in a bit over half the common stock's return, but doing so in a manner that had virtually none of the stock's risk. Remember, we purchased the bonds with a positive yield to a put just over two years out.

20

Synthetic Convertibles

The traditional view of a convertible reveals a bond with a moderate coupon, convertible into a stock. The stock is typically paying little or no dividends, with fairly high growth prospects and a good amount of volatility.

But we're not limited to this type of convertible bond. We can also develop both the income and upside our clients expect with a unique blend of non-traditional convertible-bond investments. As always, principal protection comes before everything else.

Large-Cap Upside With Synthetic Convertible Bonds

One product that we sometimes utilize at Wellesley is known as a **synthetic convertible**. Through some negotiating with large financial institutions who will act as underwriters, we can sometimes offer different options for convertible bonds using this product. While this is not new, creation of synthetic convertibles can be fruitful for the client who gets in on a well-timed, carefully constructed deal.

What Is a Synthetic Convertible?

Much as the name would suggest, a synthetic convertible is a type of convertible bond that has been constructed, for lack of a better term. Synthetic convertibles are made when a non-convertible product, like a debt note, is combined with options that together create an investment that functions very much like a regularly issued convertible bond. Investment managers like WIA can obtain these bonds by asking an investment bank to create them. The bank does this by purchasing the components, filing the necessary legal documents, and then offering the newly created bonds as a single unit to the investment manager.

The reasons why we sometimes create and then invest in a synthetic convertible for our clients are threefold. First, these synthetic convertibles are useful when we cannot find enough "regular" convertible bonds that fit the absolute-return seeking strategy that we follow based on the TRW index. The second reason is that, as you'll see in our examples, we sometimes find a wonderful company that we'd really like to invest in via convertibles, but they simply don't offer a convertible bond! Finally, the company we like may actually have a convertible bond, but its price and/or terms may not fit the TRW strategy.

In these three cases, or some combination thereof, a synthetic convertible can be exactly what the doctor ordered for us to deliver absolute returns to investors on principal-protected products like convertibles—debt instruments that give you the upside of equities without the same risk.

For those of you who have read this far, it will probably come as no surprise to you that we make it clear to our clients that not all synthetic convertibles, just as not all regularly issued convertibles, are created equal. We've had many years of experience constructing synthetic convertibles, all of which have helped us create a formula of specific terms that we believe work. Some, of course, have turned out better than others. Because highly volatile stocks are the most difficult to hedge, buying synthetic convertibles requires the willingness to sacrifice more upside. After all, the banks that issue synthetic convertibles to us aren't doing it out of a sense of charity. They need to manage their associated trading book by keeping enough of the underlying stock to pay us without losing money if the stock appreciates. But they also need to keep little enough of it so that if the stock does badly they won't end up losing money on the overall trade. The more the stock bounces around, the harder this is for the investment banks who underwrite these types of securities. In general, we prefer to buy synthetic convertibles on stocks with low-to-moderate volatility. That way, the banks won't have to charge us an arm and a leg to structure a convertible with the favorable risk/reward properties we're seeking.

Examples of Synthetic Convertibles

One of the questions you should always ask your investment advisor is if they're "eating what they cook," i.e., do they personally or does their firm invest in the products and positions that it advises its clients to invest in? With synthetic convertibles that align with our absolute-return/TRW strategy, the answer for me as a portfolio manager has been a resounding "yes!" The following are some examples of our experience investing in synthetic convertibles. And yes, I've invested in all of these myself, as well as recommended them to clients.

A Bear-Market Synthetic: UPS

For WIA and many other financial services firms back in 2006, investing in UPS was a no-brainer. They were a wonderful company with what we saw as great potential, offering good balance sheets to match. UPS was showing the kind of growth that we like to see in the companies we invest in, particularly when convertibles are involved. We thought maybe it could be another Home-Depot-style "home run." Investing at the right time (and the right price point) is key: if you're investing in a stock or bond that already carries a high price, you have a lot farther to fall—and not so much room to improve, necessarily—as you do when you buy at a more modest price and project a longer-term positive return. Their volume was growing (up 1 million parcels per day, as mentioned in a *WSJ* piece from April of 2006) and their net profits were up. There was simply little fault to find in this company.

All of the research at the time indicated that they were a strong buy, with the notes that we were looking at being rated as AA+ by Moody's and AAA by the S&P. We couldn't find a convertible bond offering that worked with our strategy, so we decided to structure a synthetic convertible for UPS in this case.

We purchased the bond on April 17, 2006, at $1,000 per bond. Issued by Deutsche Bank and Eksportfinans ASA, the bond was a six-year note (meaning it matured in six years) paying 2% interest semi-annually. The price of UPS stock at the issue date was $67, and as outlined above, we had every reason to be optimistic that the stock price would rise. Because the note was a synthetic convertible, it offered principal protection in the form of a guaranty of principal by Deutsche Bank and its affiliate (not UPS; UPS did not issue the note). We were as focused on downside protection as always but really felt we had great upside potential with UPS stock.

The market had other plans for UPS. The stock tumbled over the next two years, and by 2008, the world was firmly entrenched in the financial crisis resulting from the aftermath of the sub-prime disaster. The financial crisis was becoming a bona fide economic crisis, and the impact on firms like UPS was predictably negative. Accordingly, on October 27, 2008, when we ended up selling a majority of the notes for our clients, UPS's stock had plunged from $67 a share all the way down to $39 per share, including adjusting for dividends. Over a two-and-a-half-year period, the stock had gone down 42%. Ouch. Not a wonderful return.

But here's where the saving grace of convertibles—in this particular case, a synthetic convertible—comes into play. Because the note was principal-protected, and because it did have a 2% interest rate riding along with it, the note overall dropped in value from $1,000.00 per note to $962.80 per note. When you factor in the interest income over the two-year holding period, every holder over that time period actually made a total return of 1%.

Now, you're right: 1% isn't a fantastic return! One percent is no one's investment goal—we agree. However, where would you rather end up? Investing in a blue-chip company that analysts were clamoring for you to buy, and losing nearly 42% over a two-year period? Or, investing in the same blue chip company, in a different way, possibly giving up some of the upside if/when it occurred, but in this scenario, ending up with a 1% gain? Almost every investor we've ever met would take the latter experience. Inching forward is still forward movement, and our experience with UPS stands as a great example of the power of convertible bonds, even when they are "synthetic."

Playing It Safe With Berkshire Hathaway

Even the most uninitiated financial reader among us knows about the solid reputation of Berkshire Hathaway. That reputation, made by years of hard work and careful planning by Warren Buffet, an investor we respect immensely, is well-deserved. We were among many investors in Berkshire Hathaway, and with good reason.

Some questioned our move into Berkshire Hathaway via a synthetic convertible. Weren't we being too conservative? After all, Warren Buffet was the greatest investor of all time! Why on earth would you want to give up any of that upside! There isn't anything more rock solid than investing with Warren: "Just buy the stock," the second guessers said. We instead structured and issued a principal-protected note on the Berkshire Hathaway B shares. We felt that, even if the company was showing a positive long-term investment history, we wanted to continue to stick to the strategy embodied in the TRW and offer principal-protected opportunities. Plus, we knew what some investors might have overlooked: the great Warren Buffet's Berkshire Hathaway, when looked at in shorter intervals like five-year time periods, had actually had a number of periods it was down. We never lose our focus on protection of principal, no matter how enticing the opportunity.

On March 15 of 2005, we constructed a synthetic convertible note issued and 100% principal guaranteed by Merrill Lynch, and convertible into Berkshire B shares. The bond paid 0% interest and would be due on March 15 of 2010, so it was a bond with a five-year maturity date. The bond at issuance was worth $1,000, and the underlying stock was valued at $59.56 per share.

This is another story where the financial crisis of 2008 comes into play. Though it may smart a little bit to recall this period of uncertainty and depression in the market, we've said time and again that the market all too often will remind you of the dangers of trying to time the good patches and the bad. One of the most surefire ways of measuring performance is how investment firms do during those down periods, and how much principal they've been able to preserve for their clients—and in some cases, grow.

In 2008, the financial services industry was getting hammered.

The stock market was crashing terribly. Lehman Brothers filed for bankruptcy on September 15 of that year, triggering a chain of events. Bear Stearns had been bailed out and then subsequently bought by JP Morgan Chase in March, and we were understandably nervous about the state of the financial industry. The financial papers were awash in red ink, the news tickers reporting and feeding widespread panic. There were tremendous fears about which banks were going to make it and which weren't.

We harbored such fears about Merrill Lynch, the guarantor of our Berkshire Hathaway synthetic convertible. And while the stock for Berkshire was actually one of the only stocks to go *up* over the entirety of the crisis, it wouldn't mean much to our clients if Merrill were to go under, as we'd structured this synthetic convertible through them. Remember: synthetic convertibles are always guaranteed by the *underwriter*, not by the *company whose stock was referenced in the note*. The underwriter was, no doubt, in trouble. Merrill had written off billions of sub-prime mortgages and there were questions about what remained. The strength of Merrill's balance sheet had essentially evaporated in less than a year.

We hopped into action as fast as we could. We decided to exercise the conversion option of our note and received the common stock on September 17, 2008. At that point, clients made a 14% profit on their investment based on the value of the common stock that we then were able to immediately sell, getting us out of a potentially sticky situation much faster than if we had put the synthetic convertible back to Merrill. We acted quickly, and were able to deliver a 14% return for most clients.

This example shows the importance of having the convertible option in the product, which is why we use synthetic convertibles to structure such options where they might not otherwise be offered. This synthetic was structured so that they were convertible into the value of the underlying shares either in cash or in reinvestment in the underlying company, allowing us to get out of that note in particular and move the funds into something more desirable (cash or shares, which in the case of Berkshire Hathaway, would have been a good investment—that's not always the case).

Going Forward With Google

In the summer of 2004, Google was going public. The Internet technology company, known now for its phone operating system, search engine, email and other "cloud"-functional software, was obviously poised for growth. Technology companies are often some of the most volatile investments in any portfolio, and Google was and is no different, no matter how successful it continues to be (as of this writing, very successful). Being the risk-averse investors that we are, we wondered if there was a way that we could capitalize on Google's success without exposing our clients to the volatility that was sure to happen along the way. A principal-protected synthetic convertible note on Google was definitely an intriguing proposition for us, particularly after the IPO, when the stock went public at $85 a share and never traded below $95 during the period. In fact, on its first day of trading, "The GOOG" (as it's so fondly called, after its ticker name) closed at $100 a share.

Shortly after the IPO, WIA contacted underwriters to try to construct a five-year, principal-protected synthetic convertible note on Google. Much like the skeptics on our Berkshire Hathaway synthetic, the underwriters were almost universal in their head-shaking on this one. "Are you crazy?" they'd ask us.

Their reaction was such because the best premium they could possibly offer on a Google principal-protected synthetic convertible would be about 40%, due to the volatility of the stock. Recall earlier in this chapter when I explained how the issuer's side of these synthetic notes works? They have to hedge their bets very carefully and cover volatility. The more volatile the security, the harder and more expensive that is. They were sure that the only way that our clients would make money was if the stock went over $140 a share (40% premium implies a 40% increase in the underlying stock before conversion begins to be profitable) in the next five years. Everyone loved "the GOOG" but they thought we were nuts to take that bet.

Undeterred, we went ahead with our research and negotiations over the construction of the note until August 24, 2004, when an article in the *Washington Post* written by *Newsweek*'s Wall Street editor, Allan Sloan, came out. The article, titled "IPO Success Doesn't Justify Google's Price," read,

> Often wrong, never in doubt. Take a stand, don't duck and weave too much. ...
>
> Oh, well. I'm back from the beach and it's clear that my advice turned out to be wrong. If

you disregarded my opinion and bought Google at its $85 IPO price, you're sitting pretty, given that the stock has never traded below $95 and closed Monday at $109.40. ...

But now that the price is above the original minimum price range, I'm not in doubt. So I'll repeat what I said three weeks ago. This price is insane. And anyone buying Google as a long-term investment at $109.40 will lose money.

So I'll say it again. If you're looking at the long term, don't buy Google at this price. Wait; it will get cheaper. Sure, I was wrong about the IPO price— but at $109.40 a share, I have no doubt whatever that betting on a price fall by selling Google short is a heckuva lot better bet than buying at this price.

Buying at the right price is as important as a company's reputation, prospects, and strength when considering what to buy. It's a lot harder to make money on an investment when you've "overpaid." This was enough to give us pause. *Every* underwriter we had talked to, and now Allan Sloan, was predicting that Google would drop after hitting $109. We began to second-guess ourselves: maybe we were wrong about the long-term outlook for the stock, after all. We passed on the convertible note, moving on to other things.

It's impossible to be right 100% of the time, of course, and boy, did that maxim ever get proven with Google. The stock never went back to $109 from that day. In fact, one year later, GOOG closed at $279—a gain of over 150%. Two years later it closed at $373, up another 34%. On August 23, 2009—which would have been the five-year maturity date for the proposed note that was never to be—it closed at $445. And it keeps going up!

As we mentioned, we didn't go for Google back then. But what if we had?

Let's say that an investor bought into this on the day the *Washington Post* made its prediction, that "anyone buying Google as a long-term investment at $109.40 will lose money." How might that hypothetical investor have done? Let's say Mrs. Jones purchased a hypothetical 40% premium, five-year convertible synthetic note, like the one we were trying to construct. She could have made a return of 191%. That is absolutely not bad. In fact, it's a bit astounding, especially considering that the S&P 500 index during the same period lost 6.4%.

However, it doesn't do us any good to get bogged down in the past. We know, as experienced investment managers, that investors who waste time bemoaning mistakes and lost opportunities are not putting their focus where it should be: forward. The past can't be altered, so don't even bother looking back. Learn from mistakes and see what we can do better in the future—that's all you can do. The lesson we learned here? Never listen to so-called financial experts—especially those in the media—about the future prospects for a stock. Learn your craft, do your research, and be confident in your own instincts rather than following others.

As it turns out, we've recently gotten another opportunity to participate in the Google revolution. In 2004, there was a lot of worry about the hype surrounding Google's future prospects. Now, nearly ten years later, Google has proven its ability to execute its strategy. While the 300% annual growth years are probably gone, Google continues to innovate and expand, delivering profits to its investors. Our strategy seeks companies with upside potential, while looking for protection on downside in the event that we were wrong. A principal-protected Google play still fits this framework.

Accordingly, we were finally able to issue a principal-protected synthetic convertible in March of 2011. The note is underwritten by Goldman Sachs for a $1,000 face value per note and is backed 100% by investment-grade Goldman. The note has a five-year term, a conversion premium of 35.75% at the time of issue, and is convertible into common stock at any time at the option of the holder (remember the Berkshire Hathaway example as you keep in mind how important this option is). Since construction, the bond has been doing very well, and at the time of this writing is up about 10% of the original investment. We still have three more years left on the note to see if Google continues to do well, as the earnings projections are predicting—but in the event that it doesn't do well, again, Goldman Sachs will redeem the note at 100% of principal in accordance with the terms of the note. Having that protection there for investors is always important.

Taking a Bite out of Apple

There's no question that Apple is a technology and innovative company that's here to stay. Alternating back and forth with Exxon Mobil for the title of world's biggest company, Apple can be a controversial stock for investors, though. Many investors think that Apple will do well over the next five to seven years, continuing to innovate, and grow as a company, like Google has. Zacks, in fact, is predicting earnings to grow by 20% a year for the next five years.

Despite its success, Apple also has its detractors. This other camp thinks that Apple may fall upon hard times similar to Research In Motion, and that its iPhone could become the next BlackBerry: that is to say, obsolete. Apple needs to avoid obsolescence and continue to foster an internal culture of innovation to stay on the top of anyone's list. Whether or not they can do it is unknown. If anyone tells you they "know" where Apple is going next (or any stock for that matter), they are either foolish or lying or both.

That's why we came up with the idea of a principal-protected synthetic convertible for Apple. Underwritten by Goldman Sachs, the note carries 95% principal protection on each $1,000 bond. Each note is convertible at any time into 1.49434 shares of Apple stock by the note holder. The term of the note is seven years, with a call option by Goldman after January 26, 2018, five years after the note was originally issued. If Apple does what Zacks projects over the next five years, an investor owning one of these synthetic notes will be worth $1,996.34 for every $1,000 bond that investor owns—or a 99.6% total return and a 16% annualized return.

But it's not fair to just look at the upside, as we've said before. If Apple falls into the second camp's opinion, and the stock goes down, the investor would get back $950, or 95%, of their money. A loss of $50 is not so hard to take compared to the unbearable losses that simple shareholders would experience were the stock to plummet—some food for thought.

You may be asking why investors only get back 95% of principal with the Apple synthetic convertible. The answer is that while these deals are indeed typically structured to return 100% of principal, there is no reason why they must be done that way. As with most things in life, there are tradeoffs. Accepting a 5% reduction in guaranteed principal payment allowed us to obtain more of Apple's upside than would have been available with a traditional 100% repayment. You can think of the 95% principal guarantee in this case as similar to a larger deductible on an insurance policy in exchange for greater potential benefits.

21

Generating High-Quality Income with BDC Convertibles

With the Federal Reserve succeeding in bringing interest rates to historic lows, coupons on traditional fixed-income investments have shrunk dramatically. As investors and advisors search for new and previously untapped asset classes for sources of income, some are turning to Business Development Companies (BDCs), where annual dividend yields of up to 10% or more can be common.

A BDC is a form of publicly traded private equity. They invest in or loan money to smaller, upcoming businesses. BDCs are similar in many ways to venture capital funds. Many BDCs are set up much like closed-end investment funds but are public companies that are listed on the NYSE and NASDAQ.

BDCs started in 1980 as a means to promote investment in U.S. businesses. BDCs are pass-through structures allowing individual investors access to venture-capital-type opportunities. In these dividend-hungry times, many investors are turning to investing in BDCs because of their hefty payouts. Unlike private equity, publicly traded BDCs offer retail investors greater liquidity and, in theory, more transparency. Like real estate investment trusts (REITs), BDCs are granted favorable tax treatment in exchange for distributing at least 90% of their taxable earnings to shareholders.

But even though most BDCs pay high dividends, one negative with BDCs is they can be volatile common-stock investments. For example, Prospect Capital Corporation (NASDAQ: PSEC), a BDC, is a leading provider of flexible private debt and equity capital to middle market companies in the United States and Canada. The common stock for calendar-year 2012 ranged from $9.43 to $12.21, making the stock too volatile for investors primarily concerned with capital preservation. As with any stock, neither principal nor income is protected or guaranteed by the BDC.

A perhaps safer and better way to own BDCs may be by purchasing the BDC's convertible bond, if they have one. Previously, only a small handful of BDCs issued convertible bonds, and most of the investors were mutual funds and major financial institutions because the debt was raised as a private placement exclusively for large institutions. However, recently, more BDCs are issuing registered convertible bonds that non-institutional investors can purchase. By law, BDCs are limited to 1-to-1 debt-to-equity leverage, causing many of them to be rated investment grade by the major credit rating agencies. Banks, by contrast, typically have leverage of 8-to-1 or higher.

Let's look at one of the convertible bonds issued by Prospect Capital Corporation. The PSEC 5.5% convertible bonds due August 15, 2016, are registered and in May 2012, traded around 98 or $980 per bond. The convertible bonds have a yield to maturity of 6% in 4.25 years. The bonds' conversion premium of only about 16% enables participation in much of PSEC's upside over that time frame. While it's true that PSEC common stock yields substantially more than the bonds, the yield is not guaranteed to continue into the future, nor is shareholders' principal guaranteed by PSEC. And in the unlikely event of bankruptcy, the bondholders would have a preferential claim to the assets of the company and would need to be paid in full before anything was returned to shareholders.

22

Advisors: A User's Guide

How Well Do You Know Your Advisor?

It's important that you understand where your money is going: no one *can* or *should* care about your money more than you do. That can also apply to knowing *who* is in charge of your finances.

When choosing an investment advisor, you need to make sure that they are the right fit for you and your assets. Beyond getting recommendations from friends and colleagues and talking to them about their investment philosophy and seeing how it gels with yours, there are some simple facts that might open your eyes a little bit as to what you need to know and look out for going into the discussion.

Did you know—

- The average mutual fund portfolio manager tenure is 4.79 years, and less than 7% have at least a 15-year tenure?

- 51% of portfolio managers report *no stake* in the funds they manage, and only 10% have more than $1 million of their own money invested in those funds?

- How many times have you evaluated a fund's or manager's performance without considering if the people who built that track record are still involved in the company? Turnover matters.

It's very important that your investment firm "eats their own cooking," as we like to say at Wellesley. If they don't trust it, why should you?

Also, remember almost anyone can make money for you in a bull, or up, market. It takes a lot more skill to avoid losses during bear, or down, markets. Make sure the advisor you chose has a strong long-term track record of preserving wealth during bear stock markets.

Burned by Bernie?

By now, Bernie Madoff is a household name: we all know him as the man who engineered one of the largest Ponzi schemes in U.S. history—and who defrauded his investors to the tune of $50 *billion* or more. One of the biggest lessons that the general public has learned—or should have learned, anyway—in the wake of this scandal is that if something is too good to be true, it probably is.

My partner, Darlene Murphy, and I came up close with that lesson-in-the-making several years before the fraud came to light. That's when we heard the name "Madoff" for the very first time.

Wellesley Investment Advisors had not one but a few prospective clients who appeared to be "on the fence" about hiring us. Darlene and I met with a family office representative of one of them, in New York. We learned little about what this family was invested in—whatever it was, it sounded complex! But we dared to ask about the track record: Are you happy with this advisor? What have the returns been? That's when we heard that this advisor had delivered extremely impressive results, month in and month out. And that he was "closed to new investors" but somehow this family was lucky enough to get in. They were delighted, and that was the end of our prospecting with them.

Later, in discussions with another large prospect, we got a copy of that track record. Madoff's long-term returns showed terrific success: he hadn't had a single down year. That in and of itself isn't what set off the alarm bells, since this was before 2008 and some other top investment advisors had not had losing years, either. The thing that really got our attention was that Madoff's returns were so very *consistent*. Month after month after month of positive results. He had two or three down months in many years! The results didn't correlate with anything in particular—no certain market trends, or models. They were just up.

After our meeting, Darlene kept looking at Madoff's returns and saying that something just didn't add up. They were *too* perfect.

We didn't know there was fraud, of course, but we were deeply suspicious that something was amiss. The prospective clients, unfortunately, were all much too pleased with their personal results to make a change, and we went zero for three in front of folks who could have chosen a safer path but instead opted to stick with Bernie. I'm sorry we could not convince them otherwise.

One prospect went so far as to tell us that our investment strategy in convertible bonds wasn't sophisticated enough and didn't have enough "bells and whistles." As we now know, Madoff didn't have bells or whistles either—he just seduced clients and financial advisors with smoke and mirrors. Innocent people were ruined by this man. Such a shame.

We hope there's never another Bernie Madoff. But just in case, here are seven lessons investors should have learned from the Madoff scandal:

1. **Manager and custodian should be separate.** Madoff was both the manager and custodian of clients' assets: that should have been a very large, bright red flag. Separating the two provides insurance against fraud as well as checks and balances over the money and how it's invested.

2. **Size does not matter. Honesty and integrity matter.** Madoff ran a huge outfit—or a huge scheme, as we now know. The size of the firm does not insure the quality or safety of investment advice. Some of the worst financial blowups have happened to some of the biggest names in the business. Fraud can occur in organizations large and small; if the folks at the helm don't have integrity, it doesn't matter how big the boat is—it's still going to sink. Whether or not you go down with it is up to you.

3. **Question the investment strategy and results.** If you do not understand it, don't invest in it. Think of investments like any other service you are paying for: You're ultimately in charge of your own destiny. If you're not satisfied with the explanations on how the strategy works or the results (meaning you don't understand them or you think something is happening that doesn't make sense), don't invest with that advisor, manager, or fund. You need to be your own watchdog.

4. **Greed kills.** Forget what Gordon Gekko says—greed isn't doing anyone any good. It can ruin your life, your family's life, and your future. Slow and steady wins the race.

5. **Lack of oversight should have raised questions.** An investment firm as large as Madoff's should have had a larger CPA firm than they had doing its audits and other oversights. They avoided public scrutiny and peer review. If they had nothing to hide, they wouldn't be hiding.

6. **Look every gift horse in the mouth.** One of the things that should have alerted investors about Madoff is that he charged no fees for investment management services—which is unusual in this

business. Investors who hire a manager who offers the cheapest services but middling-to-bad returns are making a mistake—they are being penny wise and pound foolish. Why would someone offering the supposedly phenomenal returns of Madoff be working for little or no fees?

7. **If it sounds too good to be true, it probably is.** Markets go up and down. This is a rule, and it won't get broken, no matter how hard you try to talk your way around it. In the case of Bernie Madoff, my partner Darlene was right: the monthly numbers were simply too good and not true.

An Advisor's Real Job

We have already seen the results of some landmark research, conducted by the research firm, Dalbar. The studies, which focused on mutual funds, monitored mutual fund flows over a twenty-year period. The results seem to confirm the benefits of our strategy of Limited Risk Investing.

The Dalbar study of investor behavior found that while the market (as measured by the S&P 500) averaged about 8.21% per year during the period between 1993 and 2012, the *average* mutual fund investor earned only 4.25%, or barely more than half of the market! The study strongly implies that the governing variable in mutual-fund returns for *real people* in *real life* isn't performance. And, although they play a role, the things that you read about in magazines, such as sales loads and 12(b)-1 fees, don't make much of a difference to the bottom line, either.

The single most important determinant of investor-level results is, quite simply, inappropriate investor behavior. This includes the following: focusing on too short a time horizon, chasing returns, excessive switching, and unnecessary panic.

The job of a good investment advisor is not to make crackerjack investment decisions. It's not to know which way the markets are going, where interest rates are going, or to have good "intuition" (although none of that hurts). Job one of a good advisor is to help the client behave appropriately, or, put differently, to help investors avoid *inappropriate* behaviors that result in losses. Advisors who seek principal protection and seek to limit losses can buy their clients breathing room and peace of mind. Breathing room and peace of mind translate into an ability to ignore markets and focus on absolute returns. Focusing on absolute returns and ignoring what the market is doing over the short term empowers investors to do the one thing that can result in accomplishing above-average-investor-level returns: *staying the course.*

Study market history and you will learn that investing in almost any sound investing strategy for a long (twenty-year-plus) period will pay off for most investors. Historically, markets average 8% to 12%. The job of an investment advisor is to help you get there. Positive returns are a worthwhile goal, but expecting them *every single year* is not realistic. Monitoring investments is important, but placing too much emphasis on short-term performance can lead investors to bad decisions. Instead, we believe it's the advisor's role to minimize the possibility of loss through full or partial principal protection, remain disciplined, and focus on performance over full market cycles (on average six years).

Investors who allow their advisors some rein to work with the above guidelines won't be assured of outperforming the market. They should well-outperform most of the investor population, however. Not because of stellar investment recommendations (although that doesn't hurt), it will be because your advisor is helping you avoid the behavioral errors that plague investors and lead them to constant change and loss.

The One Question to Ask

> *Convertible securities allow investors to participate in a company's stock price appreciation while providing them some amount of downside protection against a decline in the underlying common stock's share price. Consequently, convertibles offer investors a defensive way to invest in equities.*
> —Brent Heck, Raymond James

At this point, we've gone over many issues that you should keep in mind when selecting a financial advisor. How long they've been in the business, if they "eat what they cook" (invest their own money in the funds that their firm pushes), and if their values and ideas are aligned with yours are just a few of the concerns that one should take into account when selecting an investment professional. But what do we think is *the* most important question to ask a financial advisor? The answer may surprise you.

While each market cycle, and each year, is different, with different events and ups and downs pushing values all over the spectrum, we think that 2008 is a pretty important year to use as a benchmark. You'll remember it as the most drastic crash in recent memory, of course, but it's emerged as more than a notorious date in history: it has become a litmus test of sorts. We would argue that the most important question to ask a financial advisor is this: ***"How much did your client portfolios fall in 2008?"***

The reason why it's important to ask the advisor this question is not so much about how much they suffered during a period where we all were suffering, but about how long it took for those portfolios to recover. As we've seen repeatedly, bear markets have ripple effects that extend far beyond the periods in which they reign. Therefore, smart investors who are investing with a limited risk investment strategy will know that they need to plan for performance in *all market cycles*. Plainly put, the danger is not just during the bear market but in what happens afterward, i.e., how long it takes to recover your initial investment. Even if you were to break even after a long period of time, you still wouldn't have grown your investments at all. In that event, your investments have not kept up with inflation, may be unable to provide a comfortable cushion for you in retirement, etc. You might have been better off just keeping it in a piggy bank! That's not a great position to be in, especially if you're planning for retirement and living out the rest of your life on an inflexible fixed income.

More bullish advisors may call this philosophy alarmist, but a closer examination of historical trends reveals that it's not mere philosophy at all—it's irrefutable fact. Following the 2000–2003 market crash, it took almost a decade for some investors to recoup. Many who had invested in high-tech or dot-com firms before that still have not seen their principal returned, more than a dozen years later. Going back even further, the losses from the 1929 stock market, for example, took twenty-five years to be fully recouped, and that's not even taking into account the loss of purchasing power that happens due to inflation over that type of time period.

Do you have twenty-five years of breathing room to see your investments break even? My guess is you don't. My father and grandfather sure didn't. But even if you did have so much mad money lying around that spending twenty-five years just getting back to even didn't bother you, still, you'd be hard pressed to say that the investments paid off. "Breaking even" doesn't exactly grow your wealth. In fact, merely breaking even means you are behind, when you factor in inflation. This is the true danger of chasing performance during a bull market and failing to plan for the inevitable bear. Investors must look at investments over full market cycles.

For argument's sake, let's say that you asked this question ("how did you do in 2008?") of a financial advisory firm and they reported that their client portfolios went down by 35% in 2008. Let's further assume that you've done a solid job for yourself so far in life, and have investible assets of around $2 million. If we carry out this hypothetical, and you were to have invested with this firm using their strategy, you would have seen a loss of $700,000 in 2008. Once you have this number, this is what you need to sit with and really evaluate. Would you have been able to live with losing that amount of money and not seeing it back for a few years, or even a few decades? No matter how risk-tolerant you might be, that's a dicey proposition. And don't be fooled by a quick come-back. If that money with that firm came back 100% in 2009, well, that's great. It doesn't negate the question, however. Unless they knew it would come back, and when (something that, by the way, convertible bonds with puts can tell you, and did tell us in 2008), the question remains. When the market falls and you hold equi-ties or mutual funds or ETFs or gold or almost any investment, no one can know how long it's going to take to come back. It could take six months, which is terrific ... or it could take sixteen years.

This is a point so important that it's worth showing you some comparisons that we believe illustrate the advantages of invest-ing with the strategy used in the Thomson Reuters Wellesley Absolute Convertible Bond Index (TRW) as opposed to chasing meteoric stock market gains (and trying to survive catastrophic downfalls). In the following chart, looking at a month-by-month comparison of the crash in 2008 and subsequent recovery in 2009, we can see that investors in the TRW, who invested using a strat-egy that accounts for absolute returns over full market cycles using convertible bonds, recovered their principal far more quickly than those who had bought the S&P.

Monthly Returns 2008 and 2009 – TRW vs S&P Total Return

	2008 – Down Year		2009 – Up Year	
	TRW	S&P	TRW	S&P
Jan	-0.54%	-6.00%	2.32%	-8.43%
Feb	0.10%	-3.25%	-1.16%	-10.65%
Mar	-0.47%	-0.43%	4.28%	8.76%
Apr	2.18%	4.87%	5.03%	9.57%
May	1.40%	1.30%	3.67%	5.59%
Jun	-3.24%	-8.43%	0.40%	0.20%
Jul	0.40%	-0.84%	6.50%	7.56%
Aug	0.91%	1.45%	1.56%	3.61%
Sep	-8.14%	-8.91%	4.25%	3.73%
Oct	-14.90%	-16.80%	-1.45%	-1.86%
Nov	-1.04%	-7.18%	1.21%	6.00%
Dec	5.65%	1.06%	3.31%	1.93%
Full Year	-17.74%	-37.00%	33.95%	26.46%

Please see descriptions of indexes in the appendix. All numbers are approximate.

The comparison clearly speaks for itself. As you can see, the TRW strategy recovered principal in about eight months. Stock market investors, assuming results along the lines of the S&P 500, have taken almost *five years* to see a return in their principal. Again this doesn't take into account the loss of purchasing power they've experienced and now have to live with by failing to at least keep pace with inflation. And no chart of numbers can measure the grief and anxiety experienced by an investor in, say, 2009 and 2010, wondering when and even *IF* their principal would ever be returned to them. None of us ever want to be in that position, yet so many of us put ourselves exactly there.

The TRW index strategy not only beat inflation in the aftermath of the 2008 crash, but it also achieved respectable returns. The value of this comparison cannot be overstated. As the investment philosophy of the TRW states, a strategy involving these types of convertible bonds is meant to minimize investment risk while taking advantage of some of the upsides of riskier vehicles like stocks. We think if you can accomplish this, you will truly have the best of both worlds. The fact that both of these worlds include the dual faces of the market—bear and bull—means that the strategy is a realistic, real-world and time-tested plan for achieving absolute returns. Investment strategies focusing solely on risky stocks and chasing performance on the S&P can't compete in this regard.

Part and parcel with talking about these loss comparisons across these strategies is the notion of *risk tolerance*. It's extremely important that an investor enter into any arrangement with their true risk tolerance top of mind. This is because, in order to manage expectations, advisors must have a true picture of what those expectations—and limitations—are. A good advisor should be able to tailor his client's investing strategy to fit his needs per his risk tolerance, something that won't be possible if a client doesn't have a true understanding of said risk tolerance himself.

Risk tolerance is something that an investor should come to terms with *before* turning his funds over to an advisor. It's not just about preferences but the reality behind those preferences. If you are older, with decreased earning power and a fixed income, it doesn't matter how okay you *think* you are with sustaining big losses during a crash. The *reality* of your situation is often that your bank balance cannot support such losses, especially if you don't have the luxury of a long time horizon in which to recover those losses (and hope to just break even, as opposed to seeing gains). A risk tolerance profile must include space for these philosophies and realities to coexist.

One hard truth of the psychology of investing is that investors think they can tolerate losses a lot better than they actually can. They claim to understand the risks going into investing, but then when they see their portfolio start to plummet, first 10%, then 20%, then 30% or more—and they realize that they're not sure when, if ever they're going to see that money come back—their perception and definition of their risk tolerance changes. This is especially dangerous because, at that point, it's not just a *theory* anymore—it's a cold, hard *reality*. This is one of the benefits of investing in a convertible-bond strategy, done right: with convertible bonds, as we've shown, investors at least can have the possibility of principal protection, if the portfolio is designed for that. With a focus on liquidity dates over a relatively short period, they'll be able to see that principal again in a short period of time, and almost better than that, they also have the knowledge that their principal is coming back to them, and when. That's assuming no defaults, of course.

As you can see, one of the main distinguishing factors of the TRW index as opposed to the S&P and other indexes like it is the lack of market timing built into the strategy. The evils of market timing are legion and have been spoken about at length already in this book; chief among those is the fact that market timing amounts to little more than gambling. I don't care how many "models" or black box formulas are employed: it's still a guessing game and should not be relied upon as a sound investment strategy. To put yourself at the mercy of market timing is to put yourself in a vulnerable position that relies on a very inexact science, if you can even call it that. And yet, just about every day, I see a new timing strategy advertised. Do they work? In our firm, our answer to that question is that yes, some timing strategies do work—until the day they don't. And they all seem to meet that day.

The Dalbar studies have illustrated that investor behavior is erratic and unreliable, whereas indexes like the TRW are a more effective, efficient, and stable strategy for performance across up and down market environments.

23

Advisor Section

This section is designed primarily for financial advisors. In only a few pages, I hope to give you a quick but constructive overview of the convertible market and Wellesley Investment Advisor's approach. Some of the topics discussed here appear in the preceding chapters of this book. I encourage *all* readers—advisors and their clients—to use the information discussed here; however, it's particularly important for advisors to understand some of the critical distinctions I make. We felt that these distinctions warranted a separate section for financial professionals.

Speaking the Language of Convertibles

Perhaps the refrain I hear most frequently from financial advisors runs something like this: "I've always meant to learn about convertibles, but they seem so complicated. How can I explain them to my clients when I can't make sense of them myself?"

In reality, convertibles aren't as abstruse as you might think. You just need to understand a few terms and concepts that are really quite intuitive once you've learned them.

Yield and Premium

In the vernacular of convertible professionals, this combination of **yield** and **premium** is used to describe the terms of any issue, especially of brand new convertible bonds. You won't spend much time with a convertible salesperson without hearing an expression along the lines of "2's up 30."

So what does "2's up 30" mean? It's convert-speak for a bond with a 2% yield and a 30% conversion premium. The yield part is straightforward enough—it works the same way it would for any other bond. As with any bond, there can be different definitions of yield, be they current yield, yield to call, yield to maturity, yield to worst, and so on. But with brand new convertibles, the price is usually 100 or very close to it, so that all the yield definitions get you pretty much the same number.

Premium, on the other hand, is a term and concept unique to convertibles. It refers to the percentage by which the bond's current market value exceeds the amount you would get for the bond if you converted it into stock **right now** and then sold the stock at the prevailing market price. One concept that can be tricky until you've heard it a few times goes like this: "high-premium" bonds usually trade at lower absolute prices and have less sensitivity to the underlying stock, while "low-premium" bonds trade at higher prices. As the premium declines, the bond trades more like the stock.

A bond described as "2's up 30" would be considered a classic hybrid convertible, offering a mix of current income, price support, and reasonable participation in the underlying shares. One good rule of thumb for how much a convertible will tend to move with the stock (also known as the "delta" of the convertible) is the difference between 100% and the bond's premium, particularly with bonds trading at relatively low premiums. Thus a bond with a low premium (say, 15%) might be expected to participate in the majority—perhaps 70%–90%—of the stock's move, while a bond with a much higher premium (say, 65%) might only participate in 20%–40% of the change in the underlying stock.

In exchange for participating in a smaller portion of the stock's upside, high-premium bonds offer the benefit of trading at lower actual prices and thus offer more attractive yields than low-premium bonds, which typically have low current yields and negative yields if the stock trades down. For example, a low-premium bond might trade at a price of 150, with a premium of 10%. It will participate in most of the underlying stock's gains from that point on, but also is susceptible to substantial losses, because you are assured only 100 at maturity, not 150. A high-premium bond, meanwhile, might trade at 90 and offer, say, a 5% yield to maturity or put, but only participate in a modest amount of the stock's near-term upside.

To recap: high premium means low price and modest equity sensitivity, a more conservative investment. Low premium means high price, big stock sensitivity, and potential for significant losses if the stock declines.

Because we only buy bonds with positive yields or, at worst, small negative yields to the next liquidity event, we avoid entering trades with a fairly large possibility of major losses. (This is not to say all our trades work the way we'd like, but our goal is the preservation of our clients' capital, as well as gains.)

Puts

The convertible world has never done a particularly good job explaining itself to the uninitiated. Perhaps that's part of the reason why there are still good opportunities waiting to be discovered! One of the most misunderstood—or ignored—features of convertibles to people outside the market is the built-in investor **put** option in most long-dated bonds.

From the issuer's point of view, it appears to suit their purposes to show debt on their financial statements as long-term. So they write convertible notes with long-dated maturities, perhaps ten to twenty years or more. But beginning in the mid-1980s and more consistently from the mid-1990s onward, the convertible market has typically demanded a way to shorten its exposure with most bond issues. It has usually done this by adding one or more put options to the bonds themselves.

A frequent misconception is that investors have to go out and buy these put options in a separate transaction after first obtaining the convertible bond. This is incorrect. The put options are intrinsic parts of the convertible security, and are outlined in the bond prospectus. For instance, a bond with a nominal twenty-year maturity might be issued with puts in years 5, 10 and 15. This means that once every five years, bondholders have a very special opportunity: the right to sell the bond back to the company. Having this feature helps protect principal by punctuating the holding of a bond with various short-term maturities, or opportunities to get out whole, while still allowing for participation in the stock's upside.

More often than not, when you see a convertible with a maturity of ten years or more, it will have at least one put that effectively shortens its lifespan. This protects you against interest rate fluctuations, credit risk, and a whole host of other risks.

You will still occasionally see long-dated convertible bonds that do not have puts. Because they lack the downside support of shorter-dated bonds, these are typically highly sensitive to changes in stock prices and interest rates. Sometimes blue-chip companies issue them because there is such demand for so-called investment-grade paper that investors willingly overpay for the cover of rating agencies (we don't do this at Wellesley). The trouble is that long-dated bonds, no matter who issues them, offer very little price support when rates rise. So, we don't recommend investing in them.

Calls

With the puts embedded in convertibles, investors have the right (but not the obligation) to sell the bonds, at certain dates, back to the issuer. This right can have tremendous value if the stock performs disappointingly.

Convertibles, particularly longer-dated ones, can also come with embedded **call** options. As with other bonds, the call option belongs to the issuer, not the investor. The issuer's right to call the bond (typically beginning three to five years after the issue date, at the issue price or a small premium) limits the investor's upside after the call date. Companies will typically exercise their right to call bonds under one of two scenarios:

1. The stock price has risen significantly. In this case, the bond is worth substantially more as a stock substitute than as a pure bond. For instance, if a bond's conversion value is 150 and the bond becomes callable at 100, the issuer would likely call the bond, thereby forcing holders to convert into stock or sell the bond in the market to someone who converts.

2. The company can refinance the bonds by issuing new debt on more advantageous terms (typically after interest rates have fallen meaningfully). We've been through some periods of declining interest rates in which bonds were being called frequently.

As with all fixed-income securities, investors must be careful not to overpay for convertible bonds in danger of being called in the near future. This is one of the areas in which professional management is especially valuable.

Conversion

Since we are dealing with convertible bonds, it's important to understand the basic concepts underlying convertibility.

Conversion Price

This is the minimum stock price at which holders are better off converting bonds into stock rather than letting the bond mature (or be called). The conversion price is set at issuance by nego-tiations between the underwriter, the company issuing the bond, and prospective buyers. For example, if a stock is trading at $20 and a convertible is issued with a 30% premium, the conversion price would be $26. Explained another way, a bond with a 30% premium, currently trading at $20, needs to rise 30% in value ($6 is 30% of $20) before it will hit the point that it might be worth converting, and as such begin travelling upward with the stock value. One frequent misconception is that you must eventually convert a convertible bond. Not true. In many cases, these bonds are never converted into stock. Another misconception is that an investor should convert bonds as soon as the stock price exceeds the conversion price. This is emphatically not so. You *never* con-vert bonds until you absolutely have to. In fact, many convertible investors will go their entire careers without actually converting a bond. More typically, investors will simply sell the bond into the open market. The buyer will ultimately be a hedge fund better equipped to extract the last bit of value. Finally, the conversion price will usually be adjusted for events such as stock splits and unusual dividends.

Conversion Ratio

This is the actual number of shares (stated in the documenta-tion for the convertible bond) into which each $1,000 face amount of convertibles can be exchanged. For instance, if a bond has a conversion price of $26, the conversion ratio would be $1,000/$26, or 38.4615 shares per bond. For most investors, it is more intuitive to discuss the conversion price (and its relationship to the current stock price) than the ratio. All you need to remember is that if you know one, you can quickly determine the other. Conversion ratios are adjusted for events such as stock splits and unusual dividends. For example, if the company declares a 2-for-1 stock split, in the case above, the conversion ratio would become 38.4615*2 or 76.923. This would, logically, imply a conversion price of $1000/76.923 or $13.

Conversion Value

This is the conversion ratio multiplied by the share price. In the last example, if the share price (after the split) was $15, conversion value would be 76.923*$15, or $1,154 per $1,000 face amount. If the bond were trading at a 20% conversion premium, the market price would be $1,154*1.2, or $1,385. In bond language, the price would be 138.5, since bonds are typically quoted as a percentage of par.

A Reminder: Don't Convert, Sell!

It's worth repeating that just because a stock rises above the conversion price, this *does not* mean you are supposed to convert the bond. The market price of the bond will account for the gain in the stock and, more important, will also retain a certain amount of premium over and above the pure stock value. This premium reflects the "insurance" value protecting the bonds from dropping below their initial value if you hold them to maturity. The premium can be significant even after the stock has risen above the conversion price; depending on the terms of the bond, it might still represent 20% or more of the bond's value. If you convert before you have to, you lose that premium.

In short—if you want to take profits, you don't convert—you sell!

The Different Types of Convertibles

Bonds

One often hears the terms "convertibles" and "convertible bonds" used interchangeably on Wall Street. Indeed, more than a few highly paid fund managers think all convertibles are bonds and have invested accordingly. The truth is a bit more involved than that.

The most typical convertible structure is indeed the bond—and just like any other kind of bond, convertible bonds represent a contractual obligation for the issuer to make timely interest and principal payments or be forced into a restructuring (often, this would mean bankruptcy). But some bonds are more bond-like than others.

What do I mean by bond-like? Essentially, I mean they are a defensive investment—a security whose value is unlikely to fall too sharply. Bonds have two general types of market risk, arising from interest-rate moves and credit deterioration. It's no secret that longer-dated bonds, all else equal, have far greater exposure to rate moves (duration) than shorter-dated ones. Similarly, the natural changes in competitive forces make longer-dated bonds generally more susceptible to credit deterioration risk than shorter ones.

But all bonds, especially longer-dated ones, are not necessarily created equal. Decades ago, it was common practice for companies to issue convertibles with twenty- and thirty-year maturities that offered investors no escape hatches during those remarkably longer periods. While we still see issues like those crop up now and then, they have been largely replaced by bonds with structures that we find far more appealing.

At Wellesley, while we aren't completely buy-and-hold investors, and while we do actively trade, we are certainly long-term investors. Central to our investing philosophy is always having one eye on what we call a "liquidity event," the next point in time when we know that, as long as the issuer remains solvent, we can recover all or most of our initial purchase price. By keeping liquidity events to within seven years (three to four years on average) from the buy date, we have found we can maintain reasonable control over interest-rate and credit risk while still giving the portfolios we manage a fair chance for significant gains.

We believe that twenty years, or even ten years, is simply too long to commit our clients' funds. While we welcome the opportunity to trade out of positions in the secondary market, we will not rely on anything beyond the issuer's obligation to remain current in its payments to us.

Usually, if we invest in a bond with a maturity of more than seven years, it is probably the case that the bond promises us a liquidity date sooner than that far-away maturity date. Typically this would be in the form of a put option. I mentioned this before, but it bears repeating, because we find this to be a great misconception: convertible bondholders do not have to go out and buy the put in a separate transaction. The put opportunities are delineated in the bond prospectus, and comprise an important part of the investor-issuer agreement. Puts have become fairly standard features in longer-dated convertible bonds. A typical structure might be a twenty-year maturity with puts in years 5, 10, and 15.

Convertible Preferred Shares

While bonds dominate the convertible market, they are by no means the only convertible structure offered. Companies have long used convertible preferred shares—typically offering investors higher yields and lower conversion premiums than bonds—to raise money. Financial issuers are especially likely to issue convertible preferred stock because it counts as equity capital (thus improving the balance sheet for regulatory purposes). In the spring of 2008, financial firms raised about $30 billion by issuing convertible preferred shares.

A common mistake many investors who wish to invest in "convertibles" make is to confuse convertible preferred with convertible bonds. The former are shares of preferred stock that are convertible into shares of common stock. They are not bonds, by any definition, and the only thing they share with convertible bonds is the convertibility aspect. This seems obvious, but in working with clients over many years, I've learned that many people confuse the two, and even professionals will tend to lump them together in casual conversation. But they are quite distinct.

As stock, preferred shares rank higher than common shares, obviously but distinctly lower than bonds in an issuer's capital structure. Failure to make a timely payment on even the most junior debt security (i.e., bonds) typically forces a company into a restructuring, usually bankruptcy. There are no such consequences for failing to pay dividends on preferred shares, however. The only constraint brought on by preferred shares is that a company cannot pay dividends to common shareholders if it is not making good on its preferred obligations.

Because our investing philosophy begins with a focus on capital preservation, convertible preferred shares simply do not fit into the vision. Our strategy revolves around a visible, quantifiable liquidity event in every investment we make. Because preferred shares lack this downside protection, they typically pay higher current income than bonds, and this attracts buyers. At the same time, they will typically feature lower conversion premiums.

In bull markets, convertible preferred shares can often outperform their convertible-bond counterparts. They are, after all, an equity security. Many "convertible security" mutual funds and even indexes contain these shares, and so can often outperform strategies such as that followed by the TRW Index, which rigorously sticks with *bonds* with short and mid-dated liquidity events designed to protect principal. **Caveat emptor! Purchasers of convertible funds should read the fine print. Many, if not all, of** such funds, contain convertible preferred securities. This may enable good performance in bull markets but don't be fooled into thinking these funds offer any bond-like downside protection when the bear comes around.

Mandatory Preferred Shares

One type of convertible preferred that's become increasingly popular is known as a "mandatory." As the name implies, investors in these shares do not have the option of converting into common stock—they are required to. These structures typically have three-year life spans in which they pay substantially higher dividends than the underlying stock before the mandatory conversion. The convertibility is structured so that holders experience the full downside of the underlying shares but only 75%–80% of the upside. In addition, holders do not (at the end of three years) participate in any of the first 20% or so of the stock's gains.

Why would anyone buy such a seemingly inferior security? Two words: current yield. Investors like yield, and yield is easy to sell. The trouble is that while current yield is at best an imperfect yardstick for any fixed-income security, it is particularly inappropriate for mandatory preferred shares. Nonetheless, many advisors have sold these securities for more than two decades on a current-yield basis.

The following example will illustrate why current yield and mandatories do not go together well. Consider the mandatory preferred shares issued in early 2011 by Unisys. They came to market at $100 per share, promising a 6.25% annual dividend (paid quarterly) before turning into common shares in March 2014. At present, they are trading at $69.25 per share with the underlying common stock trading at $24. As long as the stock is trading below $37.43 in March 2014, holders of the mandatory preferred will be required to convert into 2.6717 shares of Unisys common stock (you can see that at $37.43, those shares will be worth exactly $100).

The current yield on these shares is better than 9% (6.25/69.25). But let's say the stock stays at $24 for the next year—an assumption that makes at least as much sense as any other. Holders of this mandatory will collect $6.25 in dividends over the year, but they will ultimately convert into common shares worth only $24*2.6717, or $64.12. So an investor who buys these mandatory shares today for $69.25 and watches the stock not move for a year would actually get back a total of $70.37 in dividends and capital. That comes out to 1.62%—a small fraction of the 9% current yield.

While this mandatory appears to be somewhat overvalued, we're not saying that the securities are necessarily mispriced. Rather, our issue with them is that they expose holders to essentially the full impact of stock losses while masquerading as conservative-seeming yield instruments. Imagine, for instance, that in our example above, Unisys stock drops by half—to $12— over the year. The holder of mandatory preferred would thus end up with common shares worth only $32.06 and would thus watch an initial $69.25 turn into just $38.31 even after dividends. If you're keeping score, that's a loss of almost 45% on an investment dressed up to look reasonably safe. Remember that with a convertible bond, a company whose stock gets cut in half over the bond's life still repays the full face value of the bonds.

So if you decide to buy a convertible preferred—and I should say again, we at Wellesley assiduously avoid them—be sure you know what you're getting into.

The Thomson Reuters Wellesley Process

Convertible bonds can be as simple or as complex as you choose to make them. At Wellesley, we believe that it's usually best to keep things simple. By keeping it simple, we mean being able to take advantage of the wonderful properties unique to convertibles without having to worry about their day-to-day correlations to a host of other markets.

But saying that our process is simple doesn't mean that it's easy. We start out by looking for bonds we'd be willing to hold until the issuer is contractually required to repay us. While we're happy to take advantage of opportunities the market gives us, we don't want to rely on them.

But what defines a bond that we'd be happy to hold for its life?

We look for clean balance sheets with relatively low leverage (this simple rule helped us avoid much of the financial carnage in 2008). Simply put, we need to be amply convinced that the issuer can service and repay the debt we are purchasing. From there, we look for a substantial operating history. We like to see rising sales and GAAP profits. We consider the industry and the company's future prospects. Because, while seeking protection of principal is rule #1, we all know that we can't grow the portfolio without some gains. Gains translate into enough movement in the underlying common to result in the convertible price going up. For that reason, we also look at the current stock price, examining a variety of P/E ratios. Most of the time, we prefer stocks trading at reasonable price/earnings multiples.

After that, of course, we review the convertible bond offer itself, visiting all the terms of the prospectus. We are looking at put dates and amounts, call provisions, coupon rates, maturity dates, yields and anything else special outlined in the prospectus. We also review the amount of the issue and any other factors that play into future liquidity of this investment. Once we identify a bond that might be interesting, we then do a calculation of the price or range of prices at which we would consider buying this bond for client portfolios. Then, we study the market and see if we can purchase these bonds for this price, or not. If the market is away, we bide our time and exercise a discipline of watch and wait until the price is right. We firmly believe that buying at the right price is just as important as picking the right company, or selling at the right price. So, often, despite our excitement over an issue that's new to our portfolios, we will sit on our hands until we can get it at that good price. At any given time, we may own over one hundred bonds for clients, with many more on our watch list.

Of course, this is a summary, but I promise you, it's not so much more complex than this. With this disarmingly simple approach, we build a portfolio of solid investments that many of our competitors, frankly, might overlook. One of the benefits of remaining fairly small is that we can buy the convertibles of smaller, profitable, reasonably priced companies and get meaningful performance from them.

The convertible bond market, in its purest sense, really is a small-issuer market. As companies grow to big-cap, blue-chip status, their stocks begin to take on some of the properties of convertibles: they pay dividends and become significantly less volatile than when they were smaller (of course, they still lack the most critical aspect of convertible bonds, the promised liquidity event). As we see it, the main point of investing in convertibles is combining downside protection with a legitimate chance at substantial capital gains, while generating income all the while. You're a lot more likely to benefit from the possibility of large gains (such as doubling your initial investment or more in a three-to-five year period) when you buy the convertibles of small- and mid-size issuers. At the same time, if you buy the right convertibles, you get comparable downside protection to that of much larger issues.

Meanwhile, many investors continue to demand so-called investment-grade ratings, despite ever-increasing evidence that rating agencies are both incompetent and subject to fatal conflicts of interest. This is particularly true in convertible bonds. But even if bonds rated "investment grade" truly were excellent credits, there are other reasons not to invest in their convertible-bond issues. In general, large-capitalization companies are not looking to issue equity, either directly or through a convertible structure. To get them to issue convertibles, underwriters generally have to make the pricing highly attractive to them (and hence unattractive to buyers). Put another way, when successful large-cap companies issue converts, they usually aren't giving away any deals. Below is an example.

Consider the three-year convertible bond issued in 2010 by Microsoft. It came to market with a 0% coupon and a 33% conversion premium. Compare that income (or lack thereof) and premium with Microsoft stock itself. At the time of the issue, Microsoft was trading at $24.67 and yielding about 2.1%, no premium: obviously if you own the stock, you are already getting every penny of the upside. At issue, investors in the Microsoft convertible note knew that if Microsoft stock appreciated 33% over three years—a very reasonable scenario for a stock whose big-growth days are now decades behind it—owners of this convertible would get back their initial investment and not a penny more. By contrast, Microsoft shareholders would get the 33% appreciation plus about 7% in aggregate dividends.

Now, if Microsoft were the sort of company whose stock might double, triple, or multiply even more in several years, but also carried a fair likelihood of significant capital losses, buying the convertible might make a lot of sense. As a relatively safe, big, slow-growth stock paying a meaningful dividend, though, the stock itself almost looks like a convertible. Paying a premium and giving up yield in that situation is a questionable decision. At Wellesley, we took a pass on this one—not worth it. But, again, investors more concerned with *ratings* than profits will buy such a bond. The theory may be that you won't get fired for owning

Microsoft. But ultimately, we decided that the Microsoft convertible was—for lack of a better phrase—for suckers.

Just for fun, though, let's see how things have gone for the Microsoft bond. With about four months remaining in its life at the time of this writing, Microsoft stock is trading slightly above $28. Between the capital gain and dividends, Microsoft stock has provided shareholders with a 20% gain over that period. Not bad. Meanwhile, the convertible is trading at 100. The return on it is exactly zero.

Just as in other areas of investing, in selecting convertible bonds, every investment is a separate decision. We are absolute cheerleaders for convertible bonds, but that doesn't mean we like every convertible bond. In this case, the point is that building a portfolio of large, overvalued issues just because they have been blessed by a ratings agency would be doing our clients a severe disservice. Instead, we look for value and opportunity in the convertibles of good, smaller companies. There, we believe we can get substantially more income and the possibility of much greater upside.

As mentioned above, one of the ways we protect the downside is by choosing our entry points carefully. When we buy a convertible, we make sure that we keep our purchase price low enough to ensure a positive yield (or, at worst, a modest negative yield for bonds we find particularly attractive) if we hold to the next liquidity event. This means that not only do we restrict our investments to mid-length convertible bonds only, avoiding preferreds and long-dated bonds, but we also make sure that we don't pay too much above 100 for any bond.

Having been careful about our entry point, we then give our trades time to work. As long as the fundamentals remain comparable to when we initiated the position, we will tend to hold on to our bonds. We don't sell just because a position is down—or up. We try to let our winners run a bit. We find that with our strategy, if you protect the downside by avoiding big losers (and in general, this is a natural property of convertibles, properly bought) you can make competitive overall returns from a handful of strong performers.

Of course, there are circumstances where we will look to sell. On the upside, we typically pare back positions that have doubled, or that have gained significantly but appear to be overextended. On the downside, we will sell when the fundamentals have deteriorated—often involving a weakened balance sheet, consecutive quarterly losses, or other "bad news" about a company.

Simple? Okay, maybe not. Definitely not easy for the novice. Our principles are simple; convertible bond management, however, is not rocket science but takes some expertise.

Using these guidelines we find that we are generally able to extract the most benefits from the naturally favorable risk/reward properties of convertibles while maintaining a disciplined risk management process. The structure of convertible bonds with short- and mid-dated liquidity events offers a highly beneficial risk/reward skew that we believe is nearly impossible to find elsewhere. Adding our experience in security selection built around a highly repeatable process has led to a track record of steady positive returns over full market cycles, better than both stocks and bonds.

Using Convertibles to Improve the Efficient Frontier

I attribute much of my success to my insistence on keeping things simple and my refusal to go in for Wall Street pyrotechnics. It's with great trepidation, then, that I even use a term like "efficient frontier." Like most Wall Street buzzwords, it's an expression that is not intuitive for the intelligent layperson. Someone once said, and I agree, "efficient frontier" sounds like a clean little apartment somewhere in the Wild West.

Once in a while, though, I decide that rather than fight the buzzwords and techno babble, it's easier to go along with it. So let's talk about this thing called efficient frontier and what convertibles can do to improve it.

The concept of the efficient frontier revolves around the general financial construct of risk and reward. The idea is that if your portfolio lies on an efficient frontier, you cannot improve its expected return without adding to its risk profile. If it does not lie on this frontier, you have failed, to at least some extent, to maximize returns for the risk you are taking, or, alternatively, you have failed to minimize risk for the return you are seeking. The "frontier" can be imagined as a curved line showing all the possible combinations of risk and return, each point along it representing the best possible result for that particular combo. Moving along the curve involves trading risk for return, always to get that same best result. The notion of "Modern Portfolio Theory" (about which many books have been written, so I won't bore you with another) relies on this key theory of the efficient frontier, and that investors can make trade-offs on risk and return, and their best results will be found where the X and Y coordinates form this curved line.

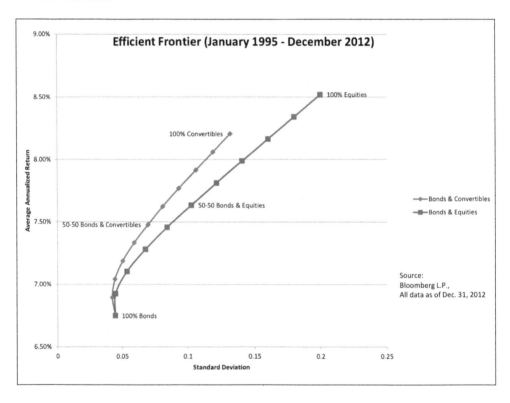

Now, I have a big problem with "risk" the way Wall Street and academics like to define it. To them, risk is uncertainty, most often measured by volatility—the extent to which an asset or portfolio moves about. This has never really made sense to me. I think of risk on a more raw, basic level—the possibility of loss. And I think most people in the real world agree with me. Of course, when you talk about loss, at some point you have to talk about what you might be losing. This is why it's inadequate to think of loss as anything other than losing your principal. Loss of purchasing power over time is surely a critical aspect as well, and is a real-life concern of every investor. However, using volatility as a proxy for risk seems to capture neither of these real-life risks, which is why I think Wall Street and the academics have all missed the boat in Modern Portfolio Theory.

Nevertheless, for the time being we will work with volatility as a measure of risk, and stay with the efficient frontier curve. Even within that flawed model, the benefit of investing in convertibles is clear. Data from Bloomberg covering the period from 1995 (when Bloomberg began tracking convertibles) to 2012 shows that investors could regularly improve returns for a given level of risk by switching from a blend of stocks and bonds to a portfolio blending traditional bonds with convertibles. Obviously, a higher weighting of convertibles led to a higher long-term return. To extend the efficient frontier curve example, the academics have found that adding convertibles to a portfolio not only makes it more "efficient" but also can actually result in a shift in the entire curve, outward, in the direction of better overall results.

This is an important point because it's often argued—erroneously, it turns out—that convertibles are an unnecessary asset class. There's nothing unique to convertibles, the thinking goes, and you can create the same payoff with a blend of stocks and bonds. It's odd that this argument has received as much general credence as it has, because it's easily disproven. Consider two $100 portfolios. One is all convertibles; the other is half stocks and half bonds. To keep the illustration simple we will stipulate that convertibles pay a 5% coupon and carry a 50% conversion premium (i.e., their conversion value is initially worth 1/1.5, or 66.67% of the bonds' face value), while traditional bonds pay 10% and stocks pay nothing. We will also assume no defaults. On the surface, it may appear that the portfolios offer equivalent income streams and outcomes.

Let's now present two scenarios. In one, stocks double, and in the second, stocks are cut in half. In the first scenario, the blended stock/bond portfolio ends up worth $155 (the $50 in stocks becomes $100, while the $50 in bonds turns into $55). The convertibles end up worth (2/1.5) or $133.33, which when combined with the coupon income gets to a total of $138.33. So convertibles provided 70% of stocks' upside in a major bull market.

Now let's look at the bear market scenario. The $50 in stocks becomes $25, so the stock/bond portfolio totals $80 with the same $55 from bonds. Meanwhile, because we are assuming no defaults, the convertible portfolio earns its $5 coupon and returns its principal for a total of $105. Here, even as the stock/bond portfolio sustains a harsh 20% loss, the convertible investor has made a 5% return.

This is simply an illustration, but it's a very important one. While you might quibble with some of the simplified numbers used, the central point is clear. **Because stocks do not offer principal protection, you cannot create a stock-bond composite portfolio equivalent to convertibles**. This is the explanation for the better efficient frontier with convertibles.

If you want to dig deeper, you can also see that even with a modest relaxation of some assumptions—such as allowing for some defaults in the convertible portfolio—the investor is still probably better off with convertibles. At the same time, it should be clear that simply buying convertibles regardless of price or quality is not a winning solution. The key, as with any type of investing, is buying the right asset at the right price. Doing this means giving yourself the potential for significant upside while keeping the downside protected. And it's not easy. But it's a lot easier—and better for sleeping well at night—than relying on the stock market.

Convertibles in Times of Market Stress

Convertibles have consistently outperformed stocks and bonds over full market cycles. We have established that. But staying invested through that full cycle can be easier said than done. I thought it would be worth spending a little time talking about the inevitable bad patches.

First, as outlined in the beginning of this book, bear markets are a fact of life. And while some bear markets are slow and protracted, they more commonly involve patches of stomach-churning downward gaps. Since we recommend convertibles for the full market cycle, you may assume that they reward investors by holding up better than stocks during the bad stretches. Is this in fact the case?

The answer is *yes*—but a qualified *yes*.

To understand what I mean, please consider Zeno's paradox,

an ancient parable concerning Achilles and the tortoise. In the paradox, the fleet warrior Achilles is racing against a tortoise, giving the tortoise a modest head start. The Greek philosopher Zeno argued that when Achilles reaches the spot at which the tortoise began the race, the tortoise will have moved ahead a certain amount. When Achilles reaches that next point, the tortoise will have advanced yet further. By this logic, though Achilles can and will shrink the distance between himself and the tortoise, he can never actually catch up.

We know, of course, that this does not make sense, yet the logic seems oddly unassailable. The problem with it is that it essentially ignores the continuous dimension of time, forcing you to think of the problem with an appealing, but incomplete, system of individual snapshots.

Similarly, when you look at how convertibles perform during short, isolated periods of market turmoil, the picture may also be a misrepresentation of the more important longer term. It's easy to point to specific instances when convertibles suffered, particularly violent ones such as the Russian credit debacle of 1998 or the global meltdown ten years later. On any given day when stocks are falling, convertibles are likely to decline, albeit at a slower rate, as well. Because convertibles are frequently marketed as defensive alternatives to stocks, down-market episodes of poor convertible performance tend to discourage prospective investors.

The reality, though, is that just like students trying to resolve Zeno's paradox of Achilles and the tortoise, investors must get past a station-to-station view and recognize that time is in fact continuous. For it is in the real world of continuous time—the "long term" in investing parlance—where convertibles, properly selected and carefully acquired, do their best work. **Every down day also brings a convertible one day closer to its next liquidity event, where principal repayment is assured as long as the company remains solvent. For an equity holder, it's just another day of looking at a losing trade.**

Investors smart enough to recognize this critical distinction may not like experiencing temporary declines in their convertible bond portfolios during bear markets. However, they understand that time, the great equalizer, is working in their favor. Some may actually welcome down markets—and they should, because these markets provide opportunities to buy convertibles well below par. These opportunities let investors lock in more attractive yields while still having the possibility of considerably better returns when stocks reverse course.

It's critical, then, to be prepared to answer investors who may be confused when they see the prices of their convertibles declining in down markets. Most convertibles have a certain degree of stock sensitivity, or "delta"—after all, that's why we buy them. In the short- and medium-term, delta means convertibles will indeed move up and down with stocks. And extended down markets can bring convertibles down below ninety cents, or even eighty cents, on the dollar—sometimes considerably lower in times of real stress. Investors should not be led to believe that this can't happen, but they should be encouraged to use these periods, if and when they occur, to invest more in the strategy.

The convertible bond market will always be quite small relative to its stock and bond cousins. Liquidity can be challenging during stretches where sellers are more plentiful and motivated than buyers. However, the market is probably a lot more robust than it was during the meltdown of 2008, when about 75% of the investors were hedge funds using leverage. That number is closer to 40% now. This means there is a much smaller likelihood of another meltdown—but also a much smaller chance of getting another 2008-style buying opportunity.

24

Some Final Thoughts

They Said It … Some Wish They Hadn't

Each January, pundits of all types ply their trade and do what they do best: make their predictions. Whether they are about politics, fashion, or finances, they're often wrong. And sometimes, they're just plain funny.

Here is a short compilation of some of the more notoriously incorrect forecasts the business and political world has produced:

"Man won't fly for a thousand years."
—Wilbur Wright, to brother Orville after a
disappointing flying experiment (1901)

"The war in Vietnam is going well and will succeed."
—Robert McNamara, U.S. Secretary of Defense
(1963)

"Everything that can be invented has been invented."
—Charles H. Duell, U.S. Patent Office director,
urging President McKinley to abolish the office
(1899)

"I cannot imagine any condition which could cause this ship to founder. I cannot conceive of any vital disaster happening to the vessel. Modern shipbuilding has gone beyond that."
—E.I. Smith, captain of the Titanic (1912)

"That is the biggest fool thing we have ever done. The bomb will never go off, and I speak as an expert in explosives."
—Admiral William Leahy to President Truman on the atomic bomb (1945)

"I think there is a world market for about five computers."
—Thomas J. Watson, Chairman & CEO, IBM (1943)

And, near and dear to our senses of humor at LRI:

"This Time It's Different"
—*Time Magazine Europe*, referring to the stock market boom of the 1990s (January, 2000)

The following quotes may not be as memorable or catchy, but they may help you remember the benefits of a professionally managed convertible portfolio.

"The interest income is welcome in a market where yield is becoming more important, but this option-like character of convertibles also appeals to investors."
    —*Financial Planning Magazine*, Dec. 2003

"The best thing about these babies is the asymmetric risk/return profile."
    —Jeff Seidel, Credit Suisse First Boston

"Even with this advantage, convertibles remain overlooked by many planners… They are complex and require a lot of research to understand if a specific issue is a good buy."
    —Ray Benton, Lincoln Financial Advisors

"[Convertibles] have a natural appeal after bear markets, because you can dip your toes into the stock market without having to dive in head first until you're ready."
    —Ray Benton, Lincoln Financial Advisors

"Convertibles are not nearly as simple as they might seem. In fact, they really can be quite complex."
—Susan Hirshman, JP Morgan Fleming Asset Management

"Advisors contemplating adding convertible securities or mutual funds to client portfolios encounter an entirely new lexicon, full of terms like "co-co" and "no-no.""
—*Financial Planning Magazine*

"If you try to buy individual [convertible] securities, you'd better know what you are doing."
—Ray Benton, Lincoln Financial Advisors

"The fact that many advisers do shun the convertibles arena can actually create opportunities."
—Ted Everett, manager of the Oppenheimer Convertible Securities Fund

"[I put clients into convertibles] who come to me and complain that they can't sleep at night because they're worried about the stock market and a lack of income. People may be wary of things they've never dealt with, but I look at this as a kind of built-in portfolio insurance for uncertain markets."
—Robert McLeod, an Alabama based advisor

Simple Rules for Excellence

Investing is anything but simple. Don't worry, you're not the only one who is confused from time to time! But hopefully, that's what you have your trusted advisor for—to help you weather the storm of market uncertainty. Remember: If you're ever unclear about something—just ask your advisor. They should have nothing to hide!

Apart from knowing when to ask for help, we like to supply our clients with a few simple rules for excellence in investing:

Never chase performance. Your friends and neighbors might have a *lot* of opinions when it comes to investing, especially after they hear that you've entered the market. Everyone has a tall tale about how much money they made when they finally guessed which big fish to bet on. They might have read an article here or there that hints to great things in the future for company XYZ. Some investment genius might be spouting his opinions on the financial news. You might know someone at work who thinks they have an inside track on something wonderful that *nobody else knows about yet*. Don't give in to temptation—keep your head down and your eyes on your own prize.

Never try to time the market. "Picking winners" or deciding when to time the market, or indexes or anything else—is *not* a sustainable investment strategy. It's gambling. If you're going to gamble, you might as well spend your money on a trip to Vegas— at least you'll get some sun and fruity cocktails out of it!

Invest with a purpose. Think about why you're investing, and how you want to do it. Take the time to talk to your advisor about your risk tolerance, what your goals are, and what you're comfortable with as a plan. Once you've made the plan, stick to it. You have your purpose—let it guide you. Review and update your goals and your risk tolerance every few years or as needed, and let your advisor know! The same ups and downs you could tolerate when you were working and collecting a salary are probably not going to persist once you step over into retirement.

Keep investing. Start investing early in life, and keep investing often. The power of compounded interest is hard to overstate. Don't let your past "mistakes" keep you from making wise decisions in the future—even if you should have started investing for retirement earlier in life, that doesn't mean that has to stop you now.

Nothing Is Certain

We wouldn't be doing you a favor by letting you keep your head in the sand about this common misconception. Just because a product is principal-protected—like convertible bonds—doesn't mean that it is entirely immune from scrutiny and sometimes abject failure.

Our firm ran into such a situation in October 2004, when a convertible bond that we favored and recommended for purchase —SPX—came under intense fire for some controversial accounting and business practices. *Barron's* came out, guns blazing, publishing an unfavorable outlook for the company. The transgressions were big deals: artificially inflating earnings, masking declining cash flow, executive turnover, insider trading, and bloated salaries for execs.

We had to sell SPX at a small loss after that. But even in that loss situation, we were vindicated in our limited-risk investment with convertibles strategy—we only lost 5.4% per bond, whereas stock investors would have lost 39% of their holdings if forced to sell at the same time. We think that's protection worth investing in, but our point really is this: anything can happen! So be prepared.

Risk Tolerance

There are several important factors to consider when reviewing your risk tolerance. It's not just a matter of what you're willing to conceive of risking, nor is it a matter of organizing an entire portfolio based around a target retirement date (though this is certainly *one* of the contributing factors).

Personal circumstances. It's important to have a sense of where you are, financially, before you even go in to meet with someone like a financial advisor. Perhaps you're young, earning a good income, and the idea of losing a few bucks in exchange for a long-term good result feels perfectly reasonable to you. Or perhaps you're at the stage of life where your net worth is a certain number, whatever that number is for you—a number that makes you say, first, "wow" and second, "I'd better not lose this." Or perhaps it's a number that's making you utter some choice expletives and wonder how you ended up here, and how are you going to get back to where you were without making circumstances worse.

It's also important to know or at least have a sense of your personal balance sheet, and what your future income and obligations are likely to be. This can be on the back of an envelope, but you should have a good idea. If it's hard to figure out, or you just need someone to walk you through it (this can be daunting, and reality can be hard to face, sometimes!), be sure to ask your advisor to help you with this, as it forms the basis of your risk tolerance, which is the underpinning of your own personal investing strategy.

This sounds very basic, and it is. But you'd be surprised how many people we've met over the years who have been talked into investments that were inappropriate to their risk tolerance. No advisor should be doing this (recommending inappropriate investments), but to be fair, if you do not do your part in being clear and honest about your personal circumstances with your advisor, he or she will have a hard time helping you.

Investment knowledge. When sitting down with a client, financial advisors will first try to assess the client's risk tolerance. Clients may say that they are highly risk-averse, but it becomes clear through further discussion that the client is just risk-averse when it comes to investments that she has little knowledge of. The opposite can also be true: if a client thinks he knows a lot about a particular vehicle, he may be more willing to take on risk for that area. But the more they know, then, sometimes the more they start to shy away from certain products. The changing landscape of an investor's investment knowledge affects their risk tolerance.

Personal background. This is a subject that hits close to home for me, as you already know. Investors are influenced by their personal history—their own or their family's experience with investments (or even the investment horror stories, or success stories, of close friends and colleagues). If you have firsthand knowledge of the devastation wrought by the Depression, for example, you're going to be a little more conservative than someone who only knows of the financial successes brought on by unusual bull markets. If you've been burned in something, or had special success with something, be sure to share that experience with your advisor.

Personal preferences. It sounds like an oversimplification, but it's undeniable: sometimes we're just wired the way that we're wired. Most people feel the pain of investment losses more acutely than they feel the pleasure of gains. There are others who love the thrill of the chase, even if it comes with great risk. The chances for great reward are what they're after. It's important to know where you are on that spectrum.

History Worth Remembering

It's easy for investors who have been exposed to the bear markets in recent memory—particularly the crashes in 2002 and 2008—to be downtrodden. The recession is still roaring in many places, and the road to recovery has been long and difficult for some investors—certainly, we are all wondering what the future holds.

But now may be a good time to take stock of the past, and see what lessons history can impart to us to help us better manage the uncertain waters of our future.

Here's what the *New York Times* had to say about the Crash of 1929 on October 29 of that year:

> Stock prices virtually collapsed yesterday, swept downward with gigantic losses in the most disastrous trading day in the stock market's history. Billions of dollars in open market values were wiped out as prices crumbled under the pressure of liquidation of securities which had to be sold at any price. ... The market on the rampage is no respecter of persons. It washed fortune after fortune away yesterday and financially crippled thousands of individuals in all parts of the world ...

The bleak news went on and on in this vein.

After the crash, the market was not done with the wrecked and ragged investors just yet. A bear market followed after a brief time of recovery. It took half an investor's typical lifetime to recover fully: only in 1954 did the market recover to levels seen before October 1929.

Today, if you were to ask investment professionals whether we'd expect to see this type of devastation again, they'd likely say *no*. And they'd probably be right. Safeguards are in place now, and the lessons of history ring in the minds of our leaders as they try to prevent such disastrous drops in short periods of time. However, those who focus on the crash alone continue to miss the larger point. The point that we're concerned with as advocates of this strategy is that when the market crashed, it stayed down and depressed for a very, very long period of time. It took a quarter-century for most people to see any part of their money again—and most people didn't make it that long.

Investing for performance following the strategy of the TRW index is designed to protect principal—not only against short-term dips and market crises, but for *long periods of market downtime* where the bear reigns and a rally is nowhere in sight. We never know what the future holds, so it's best to be prepared for anything.

One Last Story:
Investing Lessons From Blackjack

If you've picked up anything in this book, it might be that part of our philosophy about investing is that it should NOT be gambling! So you might wonder why I'm telling you a story about the gambling card game of blackjack. Read on, and you'll get it.

One day in 1968, when I was searching my college bookstore, I stumbled upon the now-famed book by Edward O. Thorp, the controversial MIT mathematician who is known in some circles as "the father of card counting." Like many of my cash-strapped student brethren, I was looking for a way to perk up my discretionary income a little bit.

I purchased the book, and read it many times. Over the next couple of years, I'd practice Dr. Thorp's system, driving my then-girlfriend (now wife!) crazy asking her to help me practice by having her deal me hand after hand of blackjack. I devoted myself to learning how to count cards, practicing against imaginary dealers for years before I finally made the move: I took a trip to Las Vegas.

I went to Vegas with $100 in hand. That may not look like much to the high roller, but it was a huge sum for me back then. I was heartbroken when all was said and done and I was down to about $20. I couldn't figure out what had happened. With my tail between my legs, I returned home to practice for months more, re-reading my magical book to try and find the keys to success. My second trip to a casino was more successful—I had a net gain of about $80. What I had started to realize was that winning at blackjack wouldn't be the get-rich-quick scheme I'd hoped for; it was going to be a slow climb at best.

On one of my next trips to Las Vegas, I witnessed something I'll never forget—that taught me a valuable lesson about gambling *and* investing, something I still think about and tell my clients to this day.

I was in the midst of a game of blackjack. Dave, the man to my left, was sitting at what's called the "third base seat"—the seat that is last to draw more cards or stay right before the dealer makes his final move. Everyone was doing well that night, it seemed—which was unusual in and of itself. Dave, in particular, didn't have a clue how to properly play blackjack and seemed to be flying blind—but doing okay. He was up a few thousand dollars that night, and felt he was on a roll.

I remember at one point, he drew a Jack and an eight against a dealer who was showing an up card of six. Even the most neophyte blackjack player should know that they should "stay" on a hard 18, which was what Dave had. But Dave hemmed and hawed for about two minutes, and signaled the dealer for a hit. The dealer called over the Pit Boss to keep an eye on things—he really didn't want to give Dave another card. The dealer, and everyone at the table who was involved in a chorus of moans and groans, knew that this was probably not going to be good news for Dave.

The dealer hit, and Dave drew a three! Twenty-one! Everyone at the table was shocked, and even more so when the dealer eventually busted. Everyone cheered and clapped Dave on the back—they were celebrating his "courage," but also the fact that since the dealer had busted, we were saved from losing to him as a whole.

This episode made me realize who the big winner in the game would always be: not Dave, and not the millions of people like him, but rather the casino and the house itself. The casinos prevail due to the fact that they rely on a consistent, low-risk strategy that is governed by probabilities, whereas gamblers are emotional and irrational creatures, with superstitions, crazy illogical "logic," and gut feelings.

Investors can be a lot like gamblers, but it doesn't mean they *have* to be. Investors who try to pick winners, time the market, or chase performance are a lot like Dave—people who could be lucky, but they could be just as unlucky, and disastrously so. If you look at investments more like casinos do, and develop long-term, conservative, logical strategies to succeed in the market, you'll understand that the best way to approach investing is to try for moderate, absolute returns with limited risk.

Anyone else is better advised to take his money and head to the casino.

25

Further Reading

Congratulations! After reading this book, you now know more than 99% of the investing public about convertibles.

If you'd like to learn even more, I suggest you read my colleague Bill Feingold's *Beating the Indexes: Investing in Convertible Bonds to Improve Performance and Reduce Risk*. As stated previously, we liked Bill's book so much that we hired him!

Bill likes to call his book a "narrative textbook." While it gets into significantly more detail than my book, it does so whenever possible by telling stories, often from Bill's own twenty-year career in convertibles. Bill's book will take you through more of the math and analytics behind convertibles without making it seem like a chore.

If you've read this book and are thinking, "Convertibles could be the right solution for MY portfolio," you can find us on the web at www.wellesleyinvestment.com or by phone at 781-416-4000. We have private wealth advisors who are ready to help you determine if investing in convertible bonds is a good fit for you.

Appendix

Indexes

The following indexes have been used as benchmark data throughout this book. Indexes do not reflect the costs of trading, management fees or other expenses. It is not possible to invest directly in an index. WIA accounts differ from an index in that they are actively managed and may include substantially fewer and different securities than those comprising an index.

Index: S&P 500 Total Return (S&P TR)
A free-float capitalization-weighted index based on the common stock prices of 500 top publicly traded American companies, as determined by S&P and considered by many to be the best representation of the market.
Source: Bloomberg data / Standard & Poor's

Index: Barclays Aggregate Bond (formerly Lehman)
A market capitalization-weighted index often used to represent investment grade bonds being traded in the United States.

The index includes Treasury securities, government agency bonds, mortgage-backed bonds, corporate bonds and a small amount of foreign bonds traded in the U.S.
Source: Bloomberg data / Barclays

Index: Bank of America-Merrill Lynch V0A0 (V0A0)

Represents all U.S. convertibles, excluding mandatory convertibles, small issues and bankruptcies.
Source: Bank of America

Index: Bank of America-Merrill Lynch B0A0 (B0A0)

Corporate Government Master – measures total return on taxable U.S. corporate and government bonds, including price and interest income based on the total mix of these bonds in the market.
Source: Bank of America

Index: Bank of America-Merrill Lynch H0A0 (H0A0)

High Yield Master II – is a commonly used index for high yield corporate bonds.
Source: Bank of America

Index: Thomson Reuters Wellesley (TRW)

TRW is the Thomson Reuters Wellesley Absolute Convertible Bond index ("TRW"). The Index is a joint venture between Thomson Reuters and Wellesley Investment Advisors. TRW is intended to represent a strategy with the goals of absolute returns and outperforming both equities and fixed income over complete market cycles deploying convertible bonds. WIA has discretion over the selection of index constituents and their weighting in the index. It is not possible to invest directly in this index, and TRW index returns do not include any management fees or transaction costs.

Source: Thomson Reuters

Index: Russell 2000 Total Return

A common benchmark for small cap investing, comprised of the 2,000 smallest capitalization companies from the Russell 3000 index.

Source: Bloomberg data / Russell Investments

About the Author

Greg Miller co-founded Wellesley Investment Advisors (WIA) in 1991 to help clients address the challenge of pursuing investment performance while protecting their portfolios. He is the firm's CEO and Co-Chief Investment Officer, and a Co–Fund Manager for the Miller Convertible Fund. Greg is the architect of the firm's investment strategy and a national expert on convertible bonds. Under his leadership, WIA has become one of America's leading investment management firms, providing hands-on convertible-bond investment management services to high-net-worth individuals, institutions, pension plans, RIAs, and other investment professionals.

Recognized as a thought leader in the investment management world, Greg is a frequent guest speaker at various investment conferences and events. He has authored numerous articles and has been profiled in various prominent investment and financial publications, including *Barron's*, *Institutional Investor*, *Investment Advisor Magazine*, and *Bloomberg*. Greg has been a guest lecturer at Babson College and Boston University. He was recently ranked a "Top 100 Independent Financial Advisor" by *Barron's* for the third

consecutive year. Greg is a CPA who practiced public accounting for over twenty years (including at PricewaterhouseCoopers),
a background he finds invaluable as the head of the investment
team at Wellesley Investment Advisors.

Greg graduated from Boston University with a Bachelor of
Science degree in Business Administration, and holds a Master
of Business Administration in Finance with high distinction from
Babson College.

Index

CPSIA information can be obtained at www.ICGtesting.com
Printed in the USA
BVOW11*1635081213

338453BV00001B/1/P

9 781939 758385